ÉAMON WILDLIFE

BOOK 3

This book is supported by Dawn Dairies

Published in Ireland by
Country House
2 Cambridge Villas
Rathmines
Dublin 6

© Country House 1987

British Library Cataloguing in Publication Data

de Buitléar, Éamon
Wildlife
Book 3
1. Natural history — Ireland — Juvenile literature
I. Title
574.9415 QH143

ISBN 0 94617 211 0

Managing editor Treasa Coady
Text editor Hugh Brazier
Designed by Design Image, Dublin
Typeset by Typeform Ltd, Dublin
Printed in Ireland by Criterion Press, Dublin

Contents

Acknowledgements

Éamon de Buitléar and the publishers wish to thank the following people and organisations for their co-operation in the preparation of this book: Deirdre Purcell, Killian Mullarney, Hugh Brazier, Richard Mills, Richard Nairn and the Irish Wildbird Conservancy, Elizabeth Sides and Dublin Zoo, Anthony McElheron and the Forest and Wildlife Service, Charles J. Haughey, Declan Doogue, Pat Hayes, John Carlos of *The Sunday Tribune,* the Ulster Trust for Nature Conservation and their education pack, Jim Hurley, Mark O'Sullivan, and Dawn Dairies for their support.

WILDLIFE FILM

by Éamon de Buitléar

Good animal behaviour films usually take a lot of time and patience. A whole film about a particular mammal, bird, insect or fish can be really difficult to make, especially since unlike people you cannot tell wild animals what to do or when to do it!

Waiting patiently

A whole series of pictures of frightened animals running away from the camera will not make a very interesting film. Therefore the first rule for the wildlife film-maker is that he or she must be a good naturalist. Being familiar with the habits of the animals is most important and knowing how to approach them without causing any disturbance is essential.

Wildlife film making is full of surprises and disappointments. Even if you plan your film really well, much of what you want to photograph is completely outside your control. I remember once spending days working where a pair of hen harriers were nesting. When I found the birds I spent a long time putting up a specially well concealed hide. Then the evening before the filming was to begin the female hen harrier was killed.

A lot of effort goes into building a hide like this.

1

Quite recently a cameraman friend of mine was filming an avocet's nest. He too had gone to a lot of trouble erecting a hide so as not to disturb this rare and elegant bird. He had several nice sequences of the avocets in the early stages of nesting and he was hoping for a complete film on the birds. Unfortunately a fox put an end to the project when it raided the nest one night and frightened the birds so badly they never returned.

This hide doesn't blend in with the natural background, but it does keep the film-maker well hidden.

But it is not all disappointment. Surprises there are a-plenty, and there is no knowing what might appear when you keep yourself hidden and remain quiet. Last year I was filming otters on an island on the west coast when a pure white hare put its head up in front of my camera. That made a nice surprise picture! A few weeks later I was lying on the bed of a river in my diving suit, taking pictures of spawning trout, when an otter swam out in front of what I was filming! So you see there are some pictures for which you can prepare plans, and other opportunities which fall into your lap when you least expect them.

Not everybody can afford to have a film camera, but you can learn to be a good naturalist. So why not play a game of being a wildlife film-maker. Learn what is happening in the countryside. Look at the many different habitats in your own locality and find out about the plants and animals living there. You could even have a go at writing a film script and then go out and observe the wildlife as if you were behind a camera. Take a sketch pad with you to record what you have seen. Good hunting!

Richard Mills

Profile 1: The Wildlife Photographer
Interview by Deirdre Purcell

For this year's *Wildlife Book* Deirdre Purcell has been roaming the country with her notebook and pencil. She has interviewed six people well known in the world of wildlife, and has written profiles of them. You will find the six profiles in the following pages.

When he was a little boy, Richard Mills was given *The Ladybird Book of Birds.* From this humblest of beginnings developed a lifelong interest. He cannot put his finger on exactly why it was birds (rather than bees, flowers or mammals) which stimulated his curiosity. He has photographed all forms of wildlife — but somehow to sit for hours, maybe a whole night, watching the comings and goings of a graceful creature like an owl and capturing them on film is the most peaceful way of passing time he can imagine.

He was in his teens when he developed an interest in photography. It was only natural that he should combine the two interests and become one of the best known nature photographers in Ireland.

It is not, of course, his full-time job. To make a living, and to support his wife and four children, he is a photographer with *The Cork Examiner*. His employers are indulgent about his hobby, and they have even discussed the possibility of publishing a regular wildlife picture in the newspaper.

On his days off he might drive to Dublin to photograph the colony of little terns which nests on the shingle strand on Bull Island. 'Little terns are declining all over the world because they tend to nest on shingle beaches and unfortunately holidaymakers often trample on their eggs. They are well camouflaged and very hard to see.' At several colonies on the east coast of Ireland there is now a special wardening scheme for their protection. The colonies are fenced off, notices have been erected and wardens are on duty during the breeding season.

Richard Mills believes that there is as much satisfaction to be gained from watching and photographing common birds in Ireland as there is from travelling to some far-flung exotic location in an attempt to shoot more colourful species. However, he does admit that to see and to film a shimmering flying pink line of flamingoes against a vivid blue sky is quite an experience. He did have such an experience in the Camargue, in southern France, where there is a large colony of these beautiful birds. To Richard, the satisfaction lies in capturing the sight on celluloid, 'I'm not really a birdwatcher as such. I won't travel hundreds of miles just to see some rare species.'

The rarest he has actually seen in this country were an American coot and a Philadelphia vireo, both of which were the first European records. Both were probably lost, blown here by strong winds which carried them off their migratory routes.

Does he think that he is a particularly patient person? 'I think so, although I tend to use a lot of bad language to myself when nothing happens after hours of waiting.' The longest he ever spent was under a bridge, in his specially built hide, waiting to photograph whatever might land on the water within range of his telephoto lenses. On that occasion, the wait was ten hours.

Quite often he does not build a hide at all, but aims his camera through his car window. He carries a special little beanbag, which he positions on the window opening of the car. He balances his camera on top of it. Telephoto lenses are very heavy and need to be supported, usually by a tripod. But it is backbreaking work, having to lug all the equipment over

4

marshy and boggy ground. Far better to drive as far as possible into a wild desolate place, settle down — and wait for the wildlife to come to you, as inevitably it will if you are quiet. After a period, the wild creatures will accept that your car is part of the landscape. The car is a ready-made hide. Birds have good hearing, but according to Richard 'they rely mainly on vision. If they cannot actually see anything moving, they are not too worried. The main thing is to move in slowly. Even when putting up a hide, you must move it in gradually.'

On the other hand, some birds are cheekier than others. 'With some birds, you can put the camera straight up and they won't take any notice of it at all. They'll even perch on it!' The birds he has in mind are the perky little robins and tits to be seen in almost all parts of Ireland, including suburban back gardens.

All photographers will tell you that film is cheap. It is because they buy it in bulk, almost by the mile. And all photographers use film as though it costs nothing at all, shooting rolls and rolls of it to get that one perfect shot. 'The trouble is, every time you're shooting, you keep on shooting, because you're always saying to yourself "well, I'll just get a better one!".' Quite often, Richard does not even bother to print the shots he has taken. 'Like cars or cameras, it's already obsolete. There's always a better one to be taken. Always room for improvement!'

As a result, he has a huge library of transparencies and negatives at home. The number may be 40,000, it may be double that. One of these days (like all of us!) he is going to get down to sorting and filing this huge store of treasure. He might even organise some of them into a book.

Like most wildlife pursuits, wildlife photography is a solitary endeavour. 'I'd say it was lonely. Even two would be a crowd. If there are two people in a car and you are trying to get a particular photograph, the other person might move at the wrong time and upset the camera. It might be nice to work with other people who have the same interest, but unfortunately there are still very few people in this country who are interested in wildlife photography.'

People who are interested in wildlife in Ireland are very lucky. The country is underpopulated and underdeveloped compared with all our European neighbours. There are still vast tracts of undisturbed wild land. It is still possible in Ireland to choose a wild spot in the countryside, maybe in the west or on an island, maybe only two miles from your city house, where you can sit all day and not see another human being. Unfortunately we are not fully alert to the threat to this priceless resource. We allow our wetlands to be drained and our bogs to be plundered in the interest of short-term gain.

Like all conservationists, Richard longs to see more money allocated to the preservation of Ireland's wild places. 'A lot of it comes down to money. The Forest and Wildlife Service should have more money. There should be more rangers, more nature reserves, more books to make people aware . . .'

Most importantly, there should be more money allocated to formal wildlife education in our schools. 'There is a lot of good work going on in the primary schools, but as soon as children move on to secondary level, that's the end of it. It seems a shame.'

Richard is half French and he lived in France as a child. He admits shamefacedly to having shot and killed various birds when he was a boy. It was culturally acceptable in France, where even songbirds are shot and eaten. Now he has reformed totally and believes that the custom is a disgrace.

His hunting instinct is now fulfilled by 'shooting' his prey on film. For anyone who would like to develop wildlife photography as a hobby, he advises that a good place to start would be the local rubbish dump. 'There are always loads of gulls and crows there, all very tame.' A pond is also a good place to practise — or any location where birds tend to congregate, and where food is readily available.

He also advises potential colleagues not to turn up their noses at the more common species. In Dublin, for instance, there are mallard there for the snapping in Saint Stephen's Green. 'You can see them just sitting there all day long, but to get a good picture of one is not easy.'

Unfortunately for young people starting off, the basic equipment is not cheap. There is little point in using an instamatic camera. 'It's so limited, you can't do anything with it.' But even the cheapest of the 35mm SLR cameras — perhaps a secondhand one to start — will cost about £100. And then you must add lenses. You would need at least one telephoto lens, and 200mm would be the minimum for any kind of satisfactory result. Such a lens, even secondhand, would cost at least as much as your camera body. But the investment would be worth it. Photographing wildlife is one of the most satisfying hobbies imaginable. It could even become a lifelong obsession, as it has for Richard Mills.

Make a Pooter
by Jim Hurley

A pooter is an instrument used by wildlife scientists to pick up tiny creatures too small to catch with fingers.

To make a pooter you will need:
one large, empty tablet container
two bendable drinking straws
one tiny piece of net curtain
sellotape
blu-tack

Assemble the pooter as shown in the drawing.

Put end A into your mouth. Scatter some tiny chips of a broken match stick, or some small seeds, under end B. Then suck air in sharply through straw A. The bits of match should fly up straw B and into the container. The net curtain filter is there to stop anything from going into your mouth.

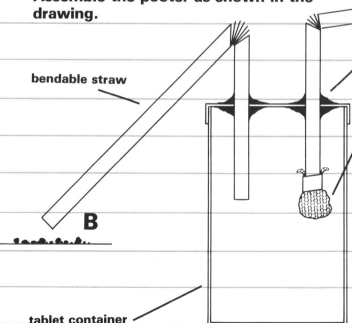

A

bendable straw

make the holes in the lid as small as possible and seal with blu-tack to make the container airtight.

net curtain filter held on with sellotape

B

When you have got your pooter working properly bring it out of doors and search for ants under stones, greenfly on rose bushes or tiny flies and beetles on the heads of flowers. Pooter them up, examine them in the container and release them again.

Why not make drawings of the different creatures you catch?

tablet container

RECENT NEWS ON WILDLIFE CONSERVATION
compiled by Richard Nairn

The wreck of the Kowloon Bridge is still just visible above the waves.

OIL KILLS SEABIRDS

When the *Kowloon Bridge*, a ship carrying iron ore, sank in storms on the west Cork coast in November 1986, few people could have known what would happen. The ship broke up below the waves during the winter and engine oil leaked from its tanks forming slicks on the sea. Over 2000 seabirds were oiled and almost all of these died either at sea or on the beaches, which were also covered in oil. Most of the dead birds were guillemots, larger relatives of the puffin, and the majority were less than one year old. Ringing recoveries showed that some came from col-

onies on the south coast of Ireland and a few from Scotland. Luckily the rest of the oil was removed from the wreck before the main breeding season of 1987 and counts of adults at the nearest colonies in County Cork showed little change from previous years. A much larger disaster was narrowly prevented.

Almost unidentifiable — an oiled guillemot.

SWANS SAVED FROM OIL

A leak of heating oil into the River Tolka in north Dublin in 1986 almost killed a flock of fifty-two mute swans. Prompt action by volunteers from the Irish Wildbird Conservancy and the Dublin Society

Oiled swans in care

for the Prevention of Cruelty to Animals brought a rescue operation in which all the affected birds were rounded up and taken into care. Those which had swallowed the oil were treated for poisoning and then began the long hard job of feeding the swans and helping them to recover. A few were too weak to survive but most recovered and were transferred to a park where they swam in the lake and preened their feathers back to shape. Eventually they were released on a north Dublin estuary. Many returned immediately to the river where the oiling incident happened.

ESTUARIES FOR RUBBISH?

A lot of the rubbish from Dublin dustbins is taken by lorry to Rogerstown, twenty kilometres north of the city, and tipped into the estuary. Many of our coastal towns and cities such as Belfast and Cork also use their nearby estuary as a convenient place to fill with rubbish.

Rubbish on the tideline

Natural saltmarsh and mudflats are covered and are no longer available to feeding birds such as waders or ducks. The dumps attract large numbers of scavenging gulls and crows. At Rogerstown dump these gulls are in the path of aircraft landing at Dublin Airport and a serious accident could happen. If the estuaries are to be saved a new plan must be prepared to separate our rubbish – to recycle the metal and glass and to burn the rest.

TERN ISLAND REBUILT

When the hydro-electric dam was built at Ardnacrusha near Limerick it raised the water level in Lough Derg causing some small islands to be covered. A colony of gulls and terns nested on Goat Island but their eggs and young were often lost when wind on the lake caused waves to wash over the tiny island. A party of volunteers from the Irish Wildbird Conservancy set about rebuilding the island in 1985. They gathered stones and gravel from the lake bed and piled them up above the level of the water. A mechanical digger was used the next year to complete the job. The terns came back and nested successfully and this is now a thriving colony again.

Common terns

RARE TROPICAL PLANTS SURVIVE

In 1985 an Irish/British expedition to Mauritius, a tiny tropical island in the Indian ocean, discovered a number of plants for which only a few individuals existed. Like the dodo these plants were doomed to extinction because their native tropical forest was almost destroyed. The expedition members built a special greenhouse where cuttings from the rare plants could be rooted and new plants produced. The aim is to re-introduce these young plants to the wild in protected nature reserves on Mauritius. Some cuttings and seeds were brought back to Ireland. Here, using advanced methods, the scientists are growing more plants which will eventually be returned to their native habitat.

Flood meadows

SHANNON FLOODLANDS SURVEYED

The mighty Shannon is the longest river in Ireland but its course to the sea is so gentle that whenever there is heavy rain it floods the fields alongside. These flood meadows or callows are very rich in wild flowers because of the fertile mud from the river and because no artificial fertiliser is used here. Insect life abounds and many rare birds such as corncrakes nest in the meadows which are cut for hay late in the summer. Otters feed in the river and nearby pools, undisturbed except by the occasional boat. Drainage of the whole river would be too expensive but some fields are being drained with new ditches. A survey of plants and birds in 1987 has identified the most important areas to be protected.

Make a Pitfall Trap
by Jim Hurley

It is often difficult to find the creepy-crawlies and other small creatures that live in rough grassland, in waste ground and along the bases of hedgerows. A good way to sample the community is to make some pitfall traps.

Method

1. Get ten glass jam jars or coffee jars, a trowel and a collection of round and flat stones.

2. Pick a line about nine metres long across the area you are going to study. At the start of your line dig a hole with the trowel and bury a jar as shown in the drawing. Repeat at one-metre intervals (or about every giant step) until all the jars are buried. Your TRAP LINE is now ready for use.

3. Put different baits in most of the jars. Use foods from the kitchen that you think the creepy-crawlies might like. I found that cheese and sausage were very successful!

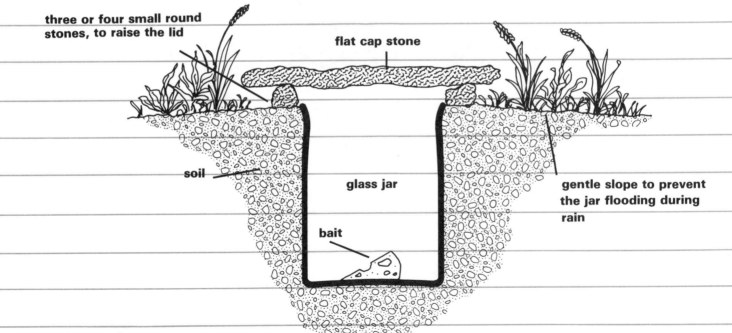

three or four small round stones, to raise the lid

flat cap stone

soil

glass jar

bait

gentle slope to prevent the jar flooding during rain

Leave some of the jars empty. These un-baited traps are called CONTROLS. A control is an experiment done to test whether another experiment works. In this case, if you catch a lot of animals in the baited jars and none in the empty jars it will prove that the animals like the bait and did not fall into the jars by accident.

4. Check your traps regularly and record your catches. Check them in the evening and then again in the early morning.

5. Release the animals as soon as you have looked at them.

Results

Copy the table below and fill in the number of creatures found in each trap.

Conclusion

What did you find out from this project? Can you say whether you got evidence to show that certain creatures are meat-eaters and others are plant-eaters? Were the animals keen on certain baits or did they just fall into the traps by chance? What did you learn from having controls? From looking at the traps morning and evening can you say which creatures go out feeding by day and which feed at night?

When you have finished this project be sure to take up all the jars and stones, fill in the holes and leave the site as you found it.

Animal	Trap No. Bait	1	2	3	4	5	6	7	8	9	10
Ground beetle											
Devil's coach horse											
Earwig											
Ant											
Slug											
Money spider											
Woodlouse											
Springtail											
Centipede											
....											
....											
....											

FOCUS ON OAK TREES

The oak is our best-known and best-loved native tree. For centuries the economy and history of Ireland were closely related to the oak forests that were the major feature of lowland vegetation from prehistoric times until the seventeenth century. Hundreds of places in Ireland are named after oak trees or oak woods. In Irish, *dair* means oak and *doire* — or derry — means an oak wood. About 1600 townland names in Ireland contain the word derry in one form or another.

Oak was used in almost every aspect of life. The trunks of the great oaks were used to build houses and bridges, fishing boats and warships, barrels and furniture. The smaller branches were converted to charcoal to smelt iron ore or used as fuel for glass-making. The bark, rich in tannin, was used for tanning leather. Even the acorns were used for feeding to pigs.

The oak tree belongs to a huge family of trees. In Ireland there are two native species of oak, the *sessile oak* and the *pedunculate oak*. The sessile oak is commoner on poor acid soils, and the woodlands of Antrim, Wicklow and Kerry are dominated by this species. The pedunculate oak grows better on richer soils, so it is more commonly found away from the mountains. There are fine woods of pedunculate oak at Abbeyleix in County Laois and at Charleville in County Offaly. Hybrids of the two species are quite common.

Identifying oak trees

An oak tree is easy to identify. Look at the shape of the tree, with its large spreading crown. Look at its rough and deeply furrowed bark. Look at the leaves with their wavy outline. Look for acorns on the tree or on the ground beneath.

But is it a sessile oak or a pedunculate oak? The pure forms are easy to tell apart, but hybrids do occur frequently, so it may not be easy to identify the species of every oak tree.

1. GENERAL SHAPE
Sessile oak tends to be straighter and taller, and has more open branches.

2. LEAVES
Both species have the well-known leaf shape, but there are differences: the pedunculate oak has a leaf which is squarer and wider at the base; sessile oak has a more distinct leaf stalk and has star-shaped clusters of hairs on the underside of the leaf.

3. ACORNS
Sessile acorns are short and conical, and sit right on the twig with hardly any stalk. Pedunculate acorns have long stalks.

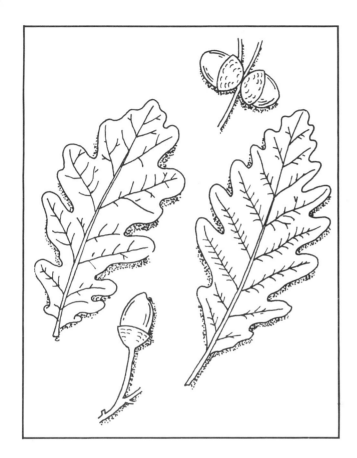

trees are probably more important today as wildlife haunts than for their timber. Many hundreds of species of insect may feed on an Irish oak tree. The caterpillars of some species occur in vast numbers, and provide an important source of food for many birds. The blue tit's breeding season is timed to take advantage of the abundant crop of caterpillars on the oak trees. Its young are in the nest when the caterpillars are most plentiful, and the baby blue tits are fed almost entirely on them.

Large oak trees also provide a home for other plants. Ferns, mosses and lichens are common on the trunks and branches of oaks. An oak wood supports a large number of flowering plants such as bluebells and wild garlic. The flowers thrive in the light shade of the oak wood. In a beech wood, where the trees cast a much deeper shadow, very few flowers grow.

The acorns provide food for mammals such as squirrels and mice, and for the larger birds such as jays and wood pigeons.

Plant an oak tree

Few people plant oaks nowadays. It is true that it is not a very suitable tree for a suburban back garden. The oak needs a large site with plenty of space for its spreading crown and roots, and it grows slowly. But it is a rewarding tree, and it is a great shame that more of them are not planted. It is hardy and easy to grow. It will grow on most types of soil and will stand up well to strong winds. If you have space, now is the time to plant your very own oak tree. Your tree may well still be alive after 400 years.

What is oak timber used for?

Oak timber is very hard and strong. In the past it was used for building houses and ships. Today it is used mainly for fine furniture and wood carving. Other specialised uses include wheel spokes and ladder rungs, where the strength of the oak is very important.

What wildlife does an oak tree support?

The oak is the best tree of all for insects. A mature oak supports more animals, and a greater variety, than any other Irish plant. Oak

Acorns ripen in October, and this is the best time of year to collect them from the ground beneath an oak tree. It is best to store them in cool, moist conditions through the winter, and then plant them in the spring. Sow more acorns than you think you need, because they will not all grow. Sow your acorns in the garden, or in a plant pot, and transplant them when they are two years old. Plant them out one or two metres apart. If there are cattle or sheep about, protect the young trees with a 'sleeve' of wire netting around each tree, or a fence around the group, until they are quite big.

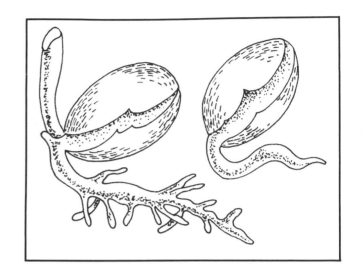

PLANT GALLS

Galls are caused by tiny wasps or flies which lay their eggs in part of the plant. Which of these can you find?

You could collect a few leaves with galls on them and keep them in a plastic tank containing some damp soil. After a few weeks or months (depending on the insect causing the gall) the adult will emerge from the gall.

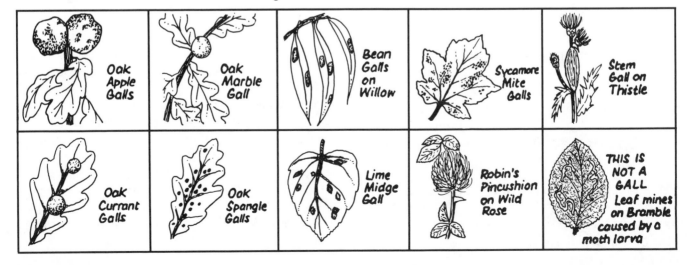

Oak Apple Galls

Oak Marble Gall

Bean Galls on Willow

Sycamore Mite Galls

Stem Gall on Thistle

Oak Currant Galls

Oak Spangle Galls

Lime Midge Gall

Robin's Pincushion on Wild Rose

THIS IS NOT A GALL Leaf mines on Bramble caused by a moth larva

How High is that Tree?

by Jim Hurley

How can you estimate the height of a tall tree?

1. Get a bamboo cane, dowel rod or other light piece of straight stick. With your arm outstretched fully, hold it vertically in your clenched fist. Close one eye and ask somebody to measure the distance from your eyelid to the point at which you are holding the stick.

2. Measure and mark the same distance from one end of the stick. Cut it across neatly at this point with a small saw. You now have a SIGHTING STICK which can be used to estimate the height of any tall object.

3. Choose a tall tree standing on its own. Hold your stick vertically, at its mid-point and at arm's length. Back away from the tree until the top of the tree is in line with the top of your stick and the base of the trunk is in line with the bottom of the stick. Be sure to keep the stick vertical and to keep your arm outstretched all the time.

4. When you are happy with the result measure the number of metres from where you are standing to the centre of the trunk. This distance will be equal to the height of the tree.

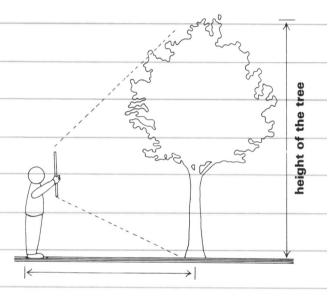

height of the tree

distance from you to the tree

5. You could repeat this project using different trees and buildings. If you turn the stick sideways it can be used to measure width as well.

Killian Mullarney

Profile 2: The Artist
Interview by Deirdre Purcell

Imagine if you were passionately interested in something, and a fairy godmother came along and waved her magic wand . . .

'Here you are, dear, go and do whatever you want for four years. Go anywhere you want or need to — and at the end of the four years I know you'll have worked hard and enjoyed yourself and there'll be a permanent record of what you did and you'll be recognised as a genius . . .' (Pouf! She disappears.)

That is not exactly what happened to Killian Mullarney. On the other hand, envious outsiders might consider that it did. From an early age he has been fascinated by birds and by drawing and painting them. And now Collins, a big publisher, has given him four years to travel all over Europe, the Middle East and North Africa, drawing every bird he sees. His drawings and paintings will be used to illustrate a definitive book to be published in 1991. And 'every bird he sees' has to be every bird that lives in or migrates through all these countries. Every single one.

'I couldn't wish for better,' he says. To hear him, you would think that it was some sort of luck that pointed Collins his way. But it was not just luck. Other bird experts consider him now to be among the top three wildlife illustrators in the world and brilliant at bird identification.

He believes that drawing birds is a marvellous help in identifying them. 'It forces a close interest. You have a much better opportunity of learning about a bird intimately than someone who is just watching. They can take in so much, but if they don't record it in some way it's impossible to remember.'

He respects his colleagues who photograph birds — and occasionally he uses a camera himself — but to him a photograph is an incomplete record of a bird. 'When you're taking photographs, stalking a bird, watching, maybe thinking of composition and of course the technical workings of the camera, you need full-time concentration and you are actually absorbing nothing of what you are seeing.' For him, photographs give details, sometimes superbly, but not the essence of the bird.

In drawing, however, he believes there is 'a direct contact where you're looking at the bird closely and sketching. Even if the sketches are rubbish, you're gaining some understanding of how the bird stands and moves and just how the whole thing works.'

Killian had no formal training in art. He believes there is no great mystery about drawing. 'I think everyone has the ability to draw. It is an ability to *see*. We can all move our hands and hold a pencil.' The problem is that when most people attempt to draw, they try to draw what they know from experience, not what they see. If they try to draw a chair it appears to be all wonky on the paper, so they give up.

But turn a chair upside-down and place it against a blank white wall and draw what you actually see, the lines, the dark bits and the white bits. Then, when you are finished, turn your paper upside-down and there will be a very creditable drawing of a chair. 'Various studies have been done on this and I think it has been shown that everyone can draw. All you need is an ability to see in an unprejudiced way, blocking out preconceived ideas.'

Killian was in a better position than most children to see things in a fresh way. He is one of a family of eleven children. At first his family lived in a remote district outside Dublin, up on the side of a mountain, so it was very difficult to send the children to school. So his mother decided to educate her children at home.

Pages from Killian Mullarney's notebook — these drawings were done while Killian was still a child.

Killian and his brothers and sisters therefore got individual attention and the particular talents of each were encouraged. Even when the family moved closer to Dublin and there were schools within reach, Mr and Mrs Mullarney found that what was on offer in them was in no way comparable to the high standards of achievement already evident in their children. They continued to educate them at home.

Being from such a large family, Killian did not miss one of the normal benefits of school, interaction with other children. 'There is no need for friends when you have so many brothers and sisters.' And he did not feel unusual. 'I didn't appreciate how unusual it was at the time.' But now he is really glad he had this great start in life.

When he did, eventually, get to a 'real' school, he was already a committed birdwatcher and a member of the Irish Wildbird Conservancy since the age of ten. It was not his unusual start, however, or his 'cissy' birdwatching habits that caused problems, but his long hair, a red rag to the classrooms full of skinhead bulls. He learned well to defend himself. 'I certainly did not lead a sheltered childhood!'

After school, although not formally trained, he spent seven years as a commercial artist. But all the time he was pursuing his first love of birds and drawing them. His expertise, both in illustrating and in identifying birds, became very well known. So much so that in 1981 he was invited to a big international 'identification meeting'. This is where he first made contact with two internationally-renowned experts on birds, Peter Grant from England and Lars Svensson from Sweden. These two are the authors of the book which will be illustrated by Killian's work.

Killian has now been working for more than a year on this exciting project. It has been most exciting in northern Scandinavia, where he spent the midsummer period. So far north, inside the Arctic Circle, the sun never dips below the horizon at midsummer, just tips it and starts to move up again.

There are so many species up there, including some which never venture south, that it is almost dizzying. Because of the unending daylight 'you're out in the field all the time until you collapse with fatigue'.

Do the birds sleep at any stage? 'Yes they do. The quietest period is from ten o'clock until midnight, but very soon after midnight they start perking up again, different species at different times. From one o'clock until five o'clock in the morning is an excellent time, because it is the period of most activity and there is so little human activity, no cars on the road.'

Some of Killian Mullarney's sketches from his 1987 note-book.

Killian does not use a hide, simply stalks in the open fields. And although he does use binoculars, he prefers a telescope on a tripod, because it leaves both hands free for drawing and he can stay quite a distance from his quarry, far enough so that the bird takes no notice of him.

Even in Scandinavia Killian found that bird habitats are being fast eroded, with felling of ancient forests and drainage of wetlands. 'It's irreplaceable. When it's gone, it's gone — unless you want to wait a thousand years.'

It is because of this concern for the conservation of natural habitats that Killian is not so opposed to the shooting of birds for sport as some other conservationists. 'The problem of vanishing wetlands (which is a huge problem in Ireland) is far more urgent than shooting. Shooting is not very nice, but it does very little damage compared to the destruction of habitat. It is not such a good idea for birdwatchers to become very anti-shooting, because ultimately the shooting people have just the same interest in preserving habitat and they form a very strong lobby.'

For the new book Killian will visit every region from Finland to the Sahara desert, from the west of Ireland to Turkey and back to the Scilly Isles. He agrees that his pursuit of birdwatching promotes such peace and personal contentment that he cannot understand why every mountaintop and bog is not covered with birdwatchers.

To anyone interested in following in his footsteps he offers encouragement. 'There's a great deal of satisfaction to be gained and a great deal of companionship. I would recommend it thoroughly as a very worthwhile outdoor pursuit that brings you in contact with interesting people. You will never be stuck for something to do, anywhere. And there are so many books and television programmes now to help you.'

For himself, he celebrates his own fortunate position. 'I have never doubted what I wanted to do. I want to watch birds and if possible make a living from it.' Out on the mountains, or even in the heart of the city, the rat-race is very far away. 'A lot of the time, very near the surface of my mind, are thoughts related to birds and not bank accounts.' With the quality of his thoughts, the bank accounts will follow.

FEEDING WILD BIRDS

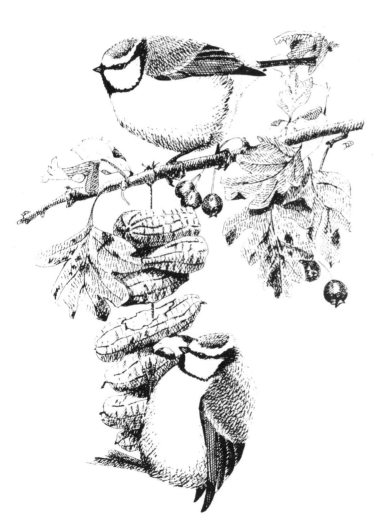

Do you put out food for the birds in your garden? It is a very good way of seeing birds and their behaviour at close quarters. It can also help the birds to survive the cold winter months. Start feeding the birds now!

What food should be given?
You can buy special bird food in a pet shop, but you don't need to do this. There are plenty of foods available. You can offer nuts, seeds, fat, bread, fruit and many other things.

Nuts
Peanuts are the most popular nuts. You can buy them in their shells, or already shelled. Or you can buy broken nuts in bulk, which works out cheaper. Brazil nuts, hazel nuts and walnuts will all be eaten if the shell is opened enough for the birds to get to the kernel.

Seeds
Almost any dry seeds from the pet shop will be eaten. These include canary, rape and hemp seed. Sunflower heads, honesty, cabbage and thistle seeds can be collected from the garden in summer, dried, and given to the birds when the weather gets cold.

Fruit

This is best put out after Christmas when the wild fruit has all been eaten. Suitable fruits are apples, pears, figs, grapes, currants and raisins, dried apricots and prunes. Dried fruit should be soaked overnight to soften it. A coconut sawn in half and hung upside-down from the branch of a tree will be welcomed eagerly by the tits. The berries of rowan, holly and hawthorn can be saved from the hedgerows. After being dried in the air, these can be stored in a cool dry place for use when food is scarce.

Fat

Don't waste any fat from the kitchen! It's a nutritious food for garden birds. Lumps of suet may be hung out. Meat trimmings, bacon rinds and table scraps will all be eaten. Bones can be hung from a branch so that the birds can get at the marrow. Or try making some tasty bird cake — the recipe is given on page 22.

Grain-based foods

There are always plenty of these in the kitchen, in the form of bread, biscuits and stale cake. You should moisten bread slightly to make it easier for the birds to swallow. Try putting some bread a little way from your bird table. This might keep the hungry starlings, crows and gulls away from the delicacies intended for the smaller garden birds.

Live foods

Mealworms can be bought at pet shops or bred at home. Robins find live food most attractive.

When should the birds be fed?

Winter is the most important time to look after garden birds. Ice and snow cover up the birds' food and water, and in severe weather the danger comes from hunger more than from the cold itself.

Feeding should start at the end of September and continue through to March or April. Do not stop too early as the female birds need plenty of food in the early spring to build up their reserves for egg laying.

Put out food regularly. If you put out food every day in the early morning, and then again in the afternoon, the garden visitors will get to know this and will be ready and waiting. Be sure to continue feeding through the winter. The birds which visit your garden can quickly come to depend on your generosity. If they suddenly find there is no food for them they could die.

Where should the food be put?

You can scatter food on the ground, or put it out on a window sill or shed roof, or hang it from trees and bushes. One easy way to present food is on a bird table. This need not be an elaborate structure — a simple tray nailed onto the top of a post or suspended from a tree will do fine. A roof to keep off the rain, and a raised rim to stop the food falling off, are useful additions.

You can hang up wire mesh containers, plastic mesh bags and seed hoppers containing nuts, seeds and other tit-bits. You can hang them from the bird table, or separately.

Cats are very common in gardens, so you must keep them away from the bird feeding area. Some birds such as song thrushes and dunnocks prefer to feed on the ground, so their food should be scattered far from cover where a cat might lie in wait. The safest areas are the centre of a lawn, path or paved area. Make sure that the bird table is out of reach of cats — at least 1.5 metres off the ground, and not too close to a tree or a wall, so that a cat cannot jump onto it.

When putting out food, spread it thinly to allow more birds to feed at the same time. Food should not be left out for too long if the birds do not eat it, as this would attract rats and mice.

What foods are not suitable?

Do not give the birds desiccated coconut, as it swells inside the birds and could be fatal. Banana skins and lemon or orange peel are also unsuitable. Foods with lots of salt in them, such as crisps or salted peanuts, should not be given. Do not put out any peanuts between April and July, as they are bad for nestlings.

Don't forget water

Birds need water for drinking and bathing all year round. A good bird bath can be made from an upside-down dustbin lid. This can be sunk into the ground, and made to look like a natural pond with stones and plants around the edge. In winter, if the lid can be raised on blocks, a small night light underneath will stop the water freezing.

RECIPE FOR BIRD CAKE

Ingredients

- A mixture of seeds, peanuts, raisins, bread or cake crumbs, grated cheese, oatmeal (in fact, any scraps you can find)
- 50-100 grams of suet or other fat

Method

Fill a yoghurt tub with the dry mixture. Melt the fat in a saucepan (be careful — it will be HOT). Pour the melted fat over the dry ingredients and stir it in. Leave to set. When it is set hard, empty the cake out on the bird table. The birds will love it.

A leaflet on feeding wild birds is available from the Irish Wildbird Conservancy. If you would like a copy, send a stamped addressed envelope to the IWC at Southview, Church Road, Greystones, County Wicklow.

Pat Hayes

Profile 3: The Sound Recordist
Interview by Deirdre Purcell

The very first wildlife sounds that Pat Hayes remembers were not wildlife sounds at all. Éamon de Buitléar's programme, *Amuigh Faoin Spéir,* was 'live' from one of the RTE studios at the time and he used to bring in turkeys, dogs, chickens — all kinds of creatures. But there were also little films from outside used in the programmes and one of the first was a film on trawling.

Pat, who was working at the time in Film Dubbing — the department which matches various sounds from its taped library — was given the task of putting sound to Éamon's film. Unfortunately he had no sounds in stock which could suggest the plopping of wet fish onto the decks of trawlers. So he recorded Éamon and various assistants as they rolled up their jerseys and slapped their own bellies. It was not scientific or authentic, but it worked!

Nevertheless, he became fascinated by the films and their subjects and always volunteered to be on duty to add the soundtrack to them. Others in Film Dubbing avoided the duty, but he sought it. 'At the time I didn't know the difference between a blackbird and a thrush.' He set about learning the difference and a whole new world opened up to him.

Before too long Éamon de Buitléar, recognising the growing interest in wildlife displayed by the sound recordist who always sought to dub his films, offered Pat a permanent job. He jumped at the chance and so began a nine-year association. His very first assignment as Éamon's soundman was to wade out into the middle of the Dargle river in County Wicklow, microphone in hand, to record the rushing sounds of the river. That tape, like all the others made over the nine-year period, is still in Éamon's library.

In the early days, filming and recording wildlife was a lot simpler than it is now, because public expectations were lower. Pat believes that wildlife films have now become so sophisticated that they are in danger of presenting a false image.

'One of the snags is that nowadays the viewer wants to see nice, bright glossy pictures of the bird or animal. He doesn't want to see a murky, dark picture. He wants everything to look beautiful.' People have been spoiled by the technical excellence of wildlife film-makers and photographers (not to speak of sound recordists). They demand a level of presentation which, he believes, does not accurately reflect the reality of life in the wild, which is often bedraggled, muddy or dull.

With Éamon he roamed the hillsides, mountain crags and wetlands of Ireland, which he found just as fascinating as the more exotic locations of Africa.

'One of the most interesting times ever was in Kerry. We went one week chasing red deer. It was absolutely fabulous.' Carrying all the heavy gear, they climbed laboriously up towards the high places they knew were inhabited by their quarry. It was a 'stop-go' mission, as are all wildlife ventures, 'sneaking it, walking it and running it' when the men were sure that they were downwind of the deer. 'You have to get the wind right and then wait in hiding with your gear set up — and sure enough, if you wait long enough, they'll drift towards you.' He succeeded in getting what he describes as 'magnificent recordings', in glowing stereo, from the bellowings and roarings of these great antlered stags.

A sound recordist may not always be so lucky. There are days of sitting forlornly in a hide, up to the knees in freezing water, tapes revolving uselessly, waiting for the sound of an animal or bird that never arrives. Quite often, the sound recordist will operate independently of the cameraperson with whom he or she works. One may get the sound or the shots desired before or after the other. Sometimes film is shot for which no suitable sound can be captured. Usually the remedy for this lies in the excellent sound archives of the BBC. On the other hand, the most frustrating thing imaginable for a sound recordist is to have captured on tape an absolutely stunning wildlife sound, for which the cameraperson can capture no matching pictures. Wild birds and animals are not good at performing to order.

The main reason for working separately is that one person disturbs wildlife less than two. And while it is possible for a camera with a telephoto lens to capture perfectly a creature who is quite a distance away, the tape recorder is less discriminating. Even the most sophisticated sound equipment cannot eliminate extraneous sound such as traffic, chainsaws, tractors, or even people's voices.

For this reason, Pat Hayes regularly found himself rising from his warm bed at times when ordinary people were going home to sleep. 'The best solution to the problem of all those background noises, tractors, chainsaws, and all the rest, is to get up really early. Certainly to be in

Pat Hayes records the sounds of the gannets while Éamon de Buitléar films.

place before dawn, so that when the birds get out of their beds they don't know you're there and the farmers are not yet ploughing their fields. A few hours after dawn it's usually a disaster.'

He says that the only places left in Ireland where you can be sure of background silence are uninhabited islands. 'There was always an annual pilgrimage to the Saltee islands in County Wexford. There are amazing colonies of seabirds there — over 20,000 birds altogether. Puffins, guillemots, razorbills, gannets, fulmars, and others.'

Pat found it more rewarding to tape the sounds of birds than those of wild animals. From the point of view of getting a weekly television programme out, birds are easier. 'You don't have to spend as much time. With badgers, foxes, all the nocturnal creatures — even bats — you have terrible trouble trying to get them.' But even to get the birds on tape often meant days of preparation, locating nests, organising extension cables, climbing to within sound range of the nest, first making sure that sitting birds were not likely to be disturbed. Then the microphone had to be camouflaged and fixed in place, disguised as a twig or a branch.

There was one nocturnal animal with whom the team had no problem at all — but that was not in Ireland. They were camping along the Omo river in Ethiopia filming the thousands of species which flourish there. They were busy filming the eagles, hawks, flamingoes, crocodiles, hippos — every creature part of a natural and flourishing ecosystem — and after the heat of the day they would fall into a deep sleep.

Then, at two o'clock every morning, Pat would be jerked out of his sleep. 'You'd sit bolt upright. There was a lion roaring outside. It was electric. You could hear the blood travelling in your veins. The first roar would be quite far away and then you'd wait thirty minutes and there'd be another one twice as close . . .'

Then there would be a long, spine-tingling wait, wondering when the next roar would come and just how close. 'You'd keep the tape recorder going the whole time, waiting — and in the meantime there would be nothing on it except insects and maybe monkeys.' When the final roar came, the earth would shake as if from thunder. 'It was amazing. They were terrific recordings.'

Pat Hayes uses a professional Nagra reel-to-reel recorder, worth around £7,000, and a professional rifle microphone which could cost between £500 and £600. His advice to any young person who is interested in recording wildlife sounds is to spend any available money on a good microphone. After that, buy the best reel-to-reel equipment which you can afford, preferably a machine that can record at a speed of 15 rpm, which is the speed normally used to record music. The frequencies emitted by wildlife, particularly by birds, are difficult to tape on anything slower. 'It's very hard to get any reasonable results at all on a cassette. They are just not capable of handling the high frequencies. Take for instance a little wren. Those tweeting frequencies are so high, they would drive the average tape recorder into distortion.'

The other piece of advice is to choose the correct time of day. 'It's to do with temperature. At certain times of the day you'll get amazing sounds and at other times you won't.' At midday the heat causes the sound to rise and it does not travel sideways. The best conditions for travelling sound are at dawn or at dusk, as any country-dweller who is familiar with the sound of evening harvesting will confirm.

Pat Hayes does not specialise any more in wildlife recording. He has gone into freelance business of his own and now specialises in feature films. But wildlife, once encountered, is never lightly put aside and he maintains a keen interest. Part of the satisfaction for anyone directly involved in recording or filming wild creatures is that it fulfils a basic hunting instinct without harm or upset to the prey. 'If you go out and get a good recording or a good picture, it satisfies that instinct without doing any damage. You just can't go out shooting and destroying willy-nilly any more. We have to think more positively. We have to protect all these things and in the process we will end up protecting ourselves.'

IONS WILDLIFE QUESTIONS WI

answered by Richard Nairn

WHY DO BIRDS MIGRATE?

Many birds such as swallows, swifts and cuckoos specialise in feeding on insects. In the cold winters of northern Europe most insects either die or hide away until the warm weather returns. So the birds must fly south of the equator where the summer lasts from October to March and where there is plenty of insect food. Swallows travel over 19,000 kilometres from Ireland to South Africa and back each year. In winter many ducks, geese and swans move into Ireland. In spring they return north to the Arctic where they can breed without disturbance from people and feed in continuous daylight during the short Arctic summer.

WHY ARE THERE NO SNAKES, MOLES OR WOODPECKERS IN IRELAND?

Today, Ireland is a small island on the western edge of Europe but 10,000 years ago it was joined to the Continent. Sea level was lower because much of the seawater was frozen in the glaciers which covered Europe in the Ice Age. As the land warmed up and the ice melted sea level rose, filling in the Irish Sea and then the channel between England and France. Animals and plants moved back north as the ice retreated with the larger mammals crossing the land bridges and migrating birds flying across the newly flooded seas. But Ireland was cut off first and some animals did not make the crossing in time. Nowadays our cool, damp climate and the lack of woodlands make Ireland unsuitable for many European animals.

HAVE MAGPIES KILLED OFF A LOT OF SONGBIRDS?

Yes, magpies do feed on the eggs and young of smaller birds but this is only one part of their diet and it is only available for a few months in the spring and summer. The rest of the time they eat insects, worms and food scraps from bird tables, dustbins and plastic refuse sacks. These artificial food sources allow more magpies to survive through the winter and their population has increased especially in towns and cities. Small birds lay a lot of eggs and some, like blackbirds, may have up to three families in a year. Most of these young ones would die naturally over the winter so that the few taken by magpies make no difference to the total population of songbirds.

ARE THERE ANY ENDANGERED ANIMALS IN IRELAND?

An endangered species is one that has decreased in numbers and is near to extinction or complete disappearance. Most of our mammals are fairly common but some like the otter and the pine marten are rare in the rest of Europe. Some of our bats are endangered because of the use of harmful chemicals. Our rarest birds are probably the corncrake, which has disappeared from most of Europe, and the roseate tern, which has declined to a few hundred pairs. There are some very rare fish such as char in Irish lakes which could be wiped out by water pollution. Many insects are endangered because the habitats such as woodlands and wetlands upon which they depend are being destroyed.

ARE THERE ANY EAGLES IN IRELAND?

At the end of the last century there were still golden eagles and white-tailed sea eagles breeding in the west of Ireland. They were easily shot by farmers who suspected them of stealing lambs. Eagles do feed on small mammals such as rabbits and hares. Some of the last eagles were poisoned when they took bait left out in dead animals. Egg collecting was also a popular activity in Victorian times and many nests were robbed. The last sea eagles nested about 1890 and the last golden eagles about 1910. A pair of Scottish golden eagles nested for a few years on the north coast of County Antrim in the 1950s but they did not stay. Occasionally there are sightings of eagles in Ireland but none have stayed to nest, possibly because of the large amount of poison which is still used in sheep farming areas.

ARE MINK HARMFUL TO IRISH WILDLIFE?

North American mink have been imported to Ireland and are kept in cages where they are farmed to produce valuable fur coats. Some mink have escaped from captivity and now live in the wild. They are small and dark (almost black) with a long furry tail and they are good swimmers. Irish rivers and lakes provide ideal conditions for mink. They feed mostly on fish and small mammals such as rats and mice. In the breeding season they will take the eggs and young of water birds such as moorhens, coots and ducks. Otters feed on very similar prey but there seems to be enough food and space for both mink and otters to live on our rivers.

FILMING THE WHITE TROUT

by Éamon de Buitléar

Sea trout, or white trout as they are known in many parts of Ireland, had always been very close to my back door. The family house was on the banks of the Dargle river in County Wicklow.

Filming underwater — can you spot the cameraman?

White trout are born in fresh water and when they are about two years old they journey downstream and swim out to sea. There is much to be learned about the life of this trout which swims and feeds around the coast. During its time in the sea it grows very quickly, and in a matter of a few months the young white trout can grow to several times its original weight.

As a subject for a film I felt that the white trout would be an excellent choice. It is a very graceful and beautifully shaped fish with a definite air of mystery about it.

Before any of the filming could begin a story would have to be written. What I wanted to do was to show the fish's early life in the river, its journey to the sea and its return again to the river where it was born. It would take an expert to write a good script, which would have to be based on scientific fact. Ken Whelan, a fishery biologist who had spent a lot of time studying freshwater fishes, was the person who had the knowledge. I was delighted when he agreed to write the story.

In order to work out the costs of the project and to plan it properly we had to work out how many days would be needed for each stage — filming, recording the sound, editing. After looking at the calendar we decided that it would take twenty-one days to shoot the film. We would then need another twenty-one days to edit the film and sound, write and record the commentary, arrange the music and finally mix all the sound tracks in the studio.

In order to tell the story accurately the activities of the trout would have to be filmed at different times of the year. The journey downstream would be filmed as the fish moved towards the sea in spring. Various other activities would be photographed during the summer, and between July and September the trouts' return journey would be filmed as they moved into the estuary on their way back to their native river.

There would be several locations including streams, lakes, rivers and coastlines. We decided that our main base would be on the River Erriff in County Mayo. Apart from the beautiful scenery in the area, the Western Regional Fisheries Board was carrying out a research programme which involved the study of migratory trout.

The scientists doing this work promised me that they would give us all the help they could. They even offered to send word immediately about anything exciting that was happening such as a shoal of fish jumping the falls or a movement of trout from the mountain lake into the streams. Having somebody on the spot to tell you what is happening can be invaluable and it can save a great amount of time and money. Instead of having to wait for days for something to happen you can be working somewhere else on other sequences and then when the message comes through you can take off and head for that new piece of excitement — hoping of course that you will make it in time!

If I were to tell you everything that happened during the making of the film this would be a very long story. We tried to keep as close as possible to our original plan but of course the fish did not always act as we wanted them to. There were other times when they surprised us by performing even better than we expected.

Every minute of film may mean hours behind the camera

Most if not all wildlife films are very much affected by weather. As we were filming our subjects in a river you can imagine how important the weather was on this occasion. There were times when we wanted flood waters, especially when the trout were due to run. At other times we wanted gin-clear streams so that we could film the activities of the baby trout. Things did not always work out the way we wanted, but eventually the work was completed pretty much on time.

I called the film *The mysterious sea trout*. I hope you see it on TV.

Ollie Otter's
FUN PAGE

If there's anything I know anything about, it's fish and other watery things. I thought you might like to join me in having some fun with them. Sharpen your pencils and . . . dive in! O.O.

ACROSS:

1. At the top of a whale's head is a _____ hole
5. An octopus has eight of these
6. A cat _____ cannot meow
8. The daily rise and fall of the ocean
12. Most fish come from an _____
14. Playful sea mammal
15. Piped ashore from the seabed near Kinsale
18. A fish's_____ helps push it through the water
19. Snakelike fish
21. Forward part of a ship
22. A sailor's cry: '_____ ho!'
23. Sea_____cannot gallop
26. A well-known film made a star of a great white _____
28. Name of the falling tide
30. _____fish have long, sharp snouts
31. What sailors ring at sea to tell time
32. Another name for 14 Across

DOWN:

2. Surfers like to ride a big _____
3. What a sailing boat needs to go
4. Largest animal in the sea
7. Some fish swim together in a _____
8. You eat this fish in a sandwich
9. A_____fish cannot bark
10. Back of a ship
11. Most fish are covered with these
13. Fish use them for breathing
16. A_____fish is named after something in the sky
17. Furry sea mammal with flippers
20. Another name for ocean
24. Shellfish that sometimes makes pearls
25. A hurricane is a bad_____
27. Kind of seaweed
29. Floating marker, often with bell or light

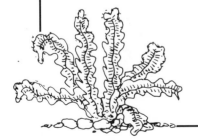

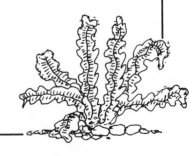

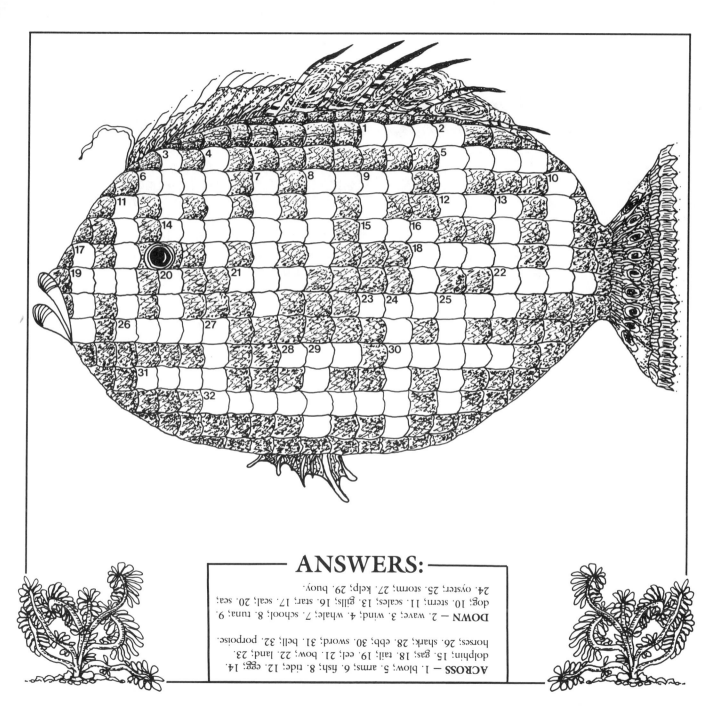

ANSWERS:

How to Make a Magic Wood

You will need:

A shoe box or similar-sized cardboard box

Some coloured transparent plastic or cellophane

Materials for making small trees and bushes (electric flex, foam sponge, bits of twig, brown paper, green crepe paper, paints)

Blu-tack or plasticine

1. Cut a hole, about 7cm x 10cm, at one end of the top of the box. Cut a peep-hole, about 1cm across, at one end of the box.

2. Make enough small trees and bushes to fill about a quarter of the base of the box. You can also make grass, dead leaves, and anything else you think would make your wood more realistic.

MAKING TREES: Cut a piece of electric flex and strip off the outer covering. To make the trunk, twist the bottom half of the wire three or four times. To make branches, separate out the strands of wire at the top of the tree. Coat the strands with glue and stick on small pieces of foam sponge for leaves.

OR: Using a piece of dead twig for the trunk, cut out branches from brown paper or cardboard. Stick these to the trunk and glue small bits of green paper onto the branches for leaves.

BUSHES can be made in the same way but with shorter trunks.

3. Plant your trees at one end of the box, fixing them in with blu-tack or plasticine.

4. Cover the hole in the top with coloured cellophane. Yellow or green will give a good effect. Shine a torch through the cellophane and view through the peep-hole — it looks magic!

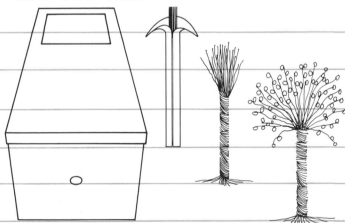

BEHIND THE SCENES AT DUBLIN ZOO

Elizabeth Sides answers some questions

Many people are fascinated by what goes on behind the scenes in the zoo. There are so many questions to ask. Where do zoo animals come from? How do you get the animals to the zoo? Are the animals tame? Where does the food come from? Is there an animal dentist? Has an animal ever escaped?

Where do zoo animals come from?

Many zoo animals are very rare in their natural habitat and should not be collected from the wild — so where do they come from? Most of the animals in Dublin Zoo come from other zoos and wildlife parks or have been born in our zoo. Rather than buying animals from each other, zoos frequently swap them or lend them to each other. Thus the vast majority of our animals have been born in captivity. However, this does not make them tame. For many animals not even the keepers can safely go in with them.

How do the animals travel?

To move animals between zoos we have to put them in boxes or crates — it all depends on their size. Crates are needed for rhinos and hippos. They have to be very strong and constructed like a horse box so that there is not too much room. This is to prevent the animals from hurting themselves. A giraffe box is like a horse box with a very tall canvas roof so that the giraffe won't hurt its head. An animal is usually coaxed into the box by putting some of its favourite food inside. If it does not behave the zoo vet may tranquillise it so that the keepers can carry it in. Animals may be flown between countries but if they are very large they come by boat and lorry. A crane is needed for getting the crate on and off the lorry.

Well-fed and contented tigers at Dublin Zoo

What do the animals eat?

An animal's diet is very important in keeping it healthy. We try hard to feed the animals food similar to what they eat in the wild. The carnivores all get meat. The large cats like the lions and tigers get approximately 3.5kg of meat a day. The herbivores are fed hay, vegetables and fruit. The elephant and the hippo, being the largest animals, get the most food: every day they each eat one or two bales of hay, 10-15kg of fruit and vegetables and 10-15kg of pellets. Monkeys are served a tray of chopped fruit, lettuce, tomatoes, hard-boiled eggs and cheese. Sealions are always fed fish and each of them eats about 5-7kg of fish a day. Penguins are also fed fish. They have to be taught to feed on dead fish, as they will not do this naturally even when born in captivity.

Where does the food come from?
All the food is bought locally and much of it comes from Smithfield market. It must be of high quality as the animals should not eat rotting fruit and vegetables. To make sure the animals get enough vitamins and trace elements most of them also get pellets which have all these ingredients. There are many kinds of pellets that are made for different animals. There is even one called monkey chow specially made in Ireland for our primates!

Do the animals visit the dentist?
Zoo animals very rarely have problems with their teeth. Why? Well, unlike us, animals do not eat very sweet foods which encourage bacteria to grow and rot their teeth. This is fortunate as most of the animals are not tame and would not let anyone inspect their teeth. The only way we can tell if an animal has a problem with its teeth is if it goes off its food and seems to be having trouble eating. This is one of the areas where the keepers play a very important role as they know their animals' eating habits very well.

Lion-tailed macaque

Do animals ever escape?
From time to time animals do escape! But fortunately they are usually captured safely and there is an amusing tale to tell at the end of the day. One day an otter escaped, but he did not like being surrounded by a lot of people trying to catch him so he hopped back into his enclosure, making everyone look very foolish! Then there was the occasion when a family of lion-tailed macaques escaped. The dominant male (the one that leads the group) was caught and put back in his enclosure and he then called the rest of his family back. Luckily for us they all obeyed. Another time a lioness found a hole in the wire that nobody had noticed. She started to take a stroll but met her keeper before she had got very far, and he managed to shoo her back. The lioness is not tame but she probably obeyed because once out of her home territory she was a little nervous.

Endangered animals

People often ask if zoos are really necessary today when there are so many superb wildlife films. They are forgetting the important role that zoos play in breeding species endangered in the wild. This is not always a simple task. For example with animals that are solitary, like cheetahs, it is necessary to separate the male and female for part of the year. We do not have enough space to do this in Dublin but it is possible at Fota in County Cork where cheetahs are bred very successfully. For other animals the right family structure may be necessary, and the males and females have to like each other for mating to occur. Dublin Zoo has a good breeding record for many animals. It is famous for its lion cubs and we regularly have Siberian tiger cubs, baby chimps, patas monkeys, giraffes and camels.

Co-operation

A problem for many zoos is that for some rare animals there are very few in captivity. This can lead to inbreeding, which means breeding between close relatives — their offspring may suffer from inherited diseases or defects. To prevent inbreeding in these species a stud book, or family tree, is kept of all the animals in captivity. It is important for zoos to notify the stud book keeper of births of these animals and when the young are old enough to leave their mother the stud book keeper tells us which zoo we should send them to. This avoids or reduces inbreeding. Many zoos, worldwide, co-operate in these breeding programmes by exchanging animals. Dublin Zoo has gorillas, orang-utans and a hippo on breeding loan from Rotterdam Zoo.

Tiger cub — a success story at Dublin Zoo

Co-operation between zoos is important for two reasons. First it helps to ensure successful breeding programmes. Secondly it reduces the value of animals. It is important that endangered animals do not have a price put on their heads as this would encourage poachers to capture the animals and sell them. After all we are trying to protect those that are left in the wild and ensure their survival by breeding them. At the same time you can enjoy seeing them in the zoo.

Anthony McElheron

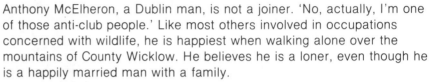
Profile 4: The Wildlife Ranger
Interview by Deirdre Purcell

Anthony McElheron, a Dublin man, is not a joiner. 'No, actually, I'm one of those anti-club people.' Like most others involved in occupations concerned with wildlife, he is happiest when walking alone over the mountains of County Wicklow. He believes he is a loner, even though he is a happily married man with a family.

For him, wildlife is a fulltime job. He is one of Ireland's forty-seven Wildlife Rangers. The rangers were appointed under the Wildlife Act to enforce its provisions and to watch over the species which need protection.

He carries out surveys on wildlife, often having to climb the highest and craggiest mountains in order to find the nesting sites of our most elusive rare birds. At present he is engaged in a survey of our smallest bird of prey, the merlin — a very difficult task, since not only is the bird small and therefore difficult to spot, it is also very secretive. There is the added problem that you never know where you might find it. 'It nests mainly in high moorland areas, sometimes on the ground and sometimes in a tree. It can occupy an old grey crow's nest or that of a magpie.' Finding one can be a matter of luck, or instinct, or experience — more likely a combination of all three.

One way to find a merlin's nest is to find the remains of its prey. First you find its 'plucking post', the place where it takes its dead prey to pluck all the feathers out, leaving them scattered around. It is a good bet that its nest will be within a short distance. This plucking post offers other valuable information. 'We can tell what kind of food the merlin is eating. In my area it's mainly lark and meadow pipit.'

The rangers get their names into the newspapers, however, not because of their constant survey work, but because of another of their duties, patrolling for poachers.

Poaching, particularly of deer, is a very lucrative exercise. There are unscrupulous people who will pay high prices for venison without asking too many questions about where or how it was obtained. So a large proportion of Anthony's time is spent patrolling the deer habitat in the Wicklow mountains, usually at night. It is quite a risky exercise, because there are guns involved.

The fines for poaching, when poachers are caught and the cases finally come to court, are not all that huge — and are not the main deterrent. 'If your rifle with telescopic sight is seized, you're talking about six or seven hundred pounds straight away. Plus your fines, plus your solicitor's costs. So a day in court can cost you the best part of £1,000. And then, if you shoot from a car, you can be disqualified from driving under another section of the Act.'

Anthony himself has to shoot deer occasionally. He does not like it, but it is necessary for proper management of the herds and of the forests in which they feed. 'I have never shot for sport. I have never shot pheasant, for example, or other game birds. I will admit there is a tremendous thrill in stalking a deer, but the actual business end of it gives me no pleasure.'

Like the other forty-six rangers, Anthony McElheron came into the wildlife service through answering a simple advertisement in the national newspapers. He had qualified as a lawyer, studying in King's Inns. Then, instead of practising law he joined an insurance company, where he stayed for seven years. He and the other rangers were appointed in November 1979.

Although he came from an indoor job, he had always had a very keen interest in wildlife, specialising in foxes and to a lesser extent in badgers. Before the foxes and the badgers, he became fascinated by wild birds. It all started when he saw a bird of prey take a little tern's chicks from its nest at Kilcoole in County Wicklow. A short while later, he saw a stoat do the same thing. 'Those incidents made me interested in the terns. I also knew there were foxes operating in the area and I began to try to find out where they were.'

It is not too difficult to find a species you are interested in if you are patient and know the signs. 'Every species leaves field signs, tracks, droppings, casts or pellets — and in that way you can build up a picture. Foxes, for instance, scent-mark their territory. That makes it quite easy to find them — it's a very distinctive smell!'

Probably the most rewarding aspect of his job for Anthony is lecturing to young people in schools. He also brings groups of children out into the forests and mountains. He shows them how to find badgers or how to read the trail left by deer — their droppings, the hair in the ferny hollow where they have lain, their hoof imprints. Even, occasionally and most excitingly, a set of shed antlers.

He believes that these are exciting times for wildlife. Of course he would love to see more funds being spent on conservation and the protection of wildlife. If he was given an elastic purse, it would be spent on specially

Anthony McElheron alone in the forest

reserved conservation areas, where all species could roam free in their natural habitat. But in the difficult economic circumstances of today's Ireland he is happy to see that interest in our natural environment is flourishing and growing. Part of the huge interest is to do with the high quality of wildlife programmes on television. All of the clubs (which he has not joined!) are doing wonderful work — the Irish Wildbird Conservancy, the Irish Deer Society, the Irish Wildlife Federation, An Taisce.

And like all who are genuinely interested in wildlife, his aim is to allow all species to live wild. He was given a fox cub once, a little female, still blind, who had been rescued by his local coalman. The coalman on his rounds had come upon a group of people about to throw an entire litter of the tiny cubs to a pack of hounds. The coalman persuaded the 'sportsmen' to sell two of the cubs to him and he brought one to Anthony McElheron. The little vixen thrived and even became house-trained. The only problem was that she had an insatiable appetite for telephone cables and every week or so poor Anthony had to make up another excuse for the telephone company, so that they would come out and repair his telephone wires. Eventually he told the truth and the telephone repair man became fascinated with Trotsky ('we called her that because she was a real red!'). He even called to repair telephones when no repairs were necessary, in order to visit his new friend.

Trotsky was returned to the wild when she was ready — at about the age of ten months. She bred successfully for two seasons in a den only two miles from her nursery home. And then Anthony and his family lost sight of her. 'She probably died a natural death. They are not all that long-lived.'

So he does not recommend taking wild animals or birds for pets. It is unnecessary and cruel. There is even a particularly vicious trade in them, for there is a large market for wild finches in Ireland and abroad. Anthony and his colleagues are aware of it and do their best to stop it, but at times it seems a losing battle.

The finches are trapped by the use of 'Dak' — a black, sticky substance smeared on perches and branches. They stick to it and are easily plucked off. After the Dak is cleaned from their feet they are inserted into the central cardboard rolls taken from toilet paper so that they cannot move their wings or struggle. Dozens of them can then be packed in bags for illegal shipping. 'When finches are tightly pinned like that and in the dark, they make no sound. It is almost impossible to detect them.'

The only hope for finches, foxes, deer and merlins is the professional vigilance of rangers like Anthony McElheron and his colleagues, assisted by the new awareness they are fostering in you and me.

JULIE, MY PET PINE MARTEN
BY MARK O'SULLIVAN, AGE 10

My name is Mark and I live in County Clare. I am very interested in wildlife, furry animals especially. I know a lot about pine martens because my dad has spent seven years studying these animals. He does research for the Forest and Wildlife Service. Very little was known about pine martens in Ireland before my dad's work began. But now we know what they eat, what their habits are, and where they live.

A pine marten we've named Julie lives with us now. Julie is a beautiful animal. We got her from a man who found her near a road where her mother had been killed. She was about two months old then and looked just like a little kitten. She is chocolate brown with a yellow throat patch, and she has rounded ears with creamy tops.

I feed Julie on scraps from the table. She eats cornflakes, potatoes and scraps of meat. But she especially likes strawberry jam. My mum says she has a sweet tooth just like me! If Julie lived in the wild she would eat berries, small mammals and birds, nuts, insects, snails and worms.

Dad says that pine martens were living in Ireland long before people came to live here. Their name in Irish is cat crainn, which means tree cat.

People once hunted and trapped martens for their fur. The fur was used to make women's coats. But now we have a law protecting the martens. We need this law because the animal is now very rare. It lives only in a few places in the west of the country.

I will not keep Julie for very long. We are teaching her to find her own food outside. Then, when she is old enough to fend for herself, she can go back to the wild. I will miss her, though, as we have a lot of fun together. We include my dog Chips in our games, and Chips and Julie love playing with each other. They have some great chases!

As I've already said, I will miss her very much when I set her free. And I'm sure she will miss strawberry jam!

STUDYING PUFFINS

by Hugh Brazier

This puffin has been ringed and is now ready to be released.

What better place to spend your summer holidays than an uninhabited island? Not a desert island like Robinson Crusoe's, but one of the many hundreds of islands off the west coast of Ireland. No traffic, no pollution, no people, no noise except the sound of the wind and the waves — and the cries of the seabirds.

Puffin Island in County Kerry is a nature reserve owned by the Irish Wildbird Conservancy. It is steep and rocky and surrounded by dangerous cliffs. There are no trees or bushes, and no streams to provide drinking water. If you want to stay on Puffin Island you must take a tent and all the food and water you will need for your stay. It is a long way from the comforts of home, but is an ideal place to spend a fortnight in June.

Puffin Island is home to over 10,000 puffins and many other seabirds as well. On a fine summer evening the puffin colony is a hive of activity. Evening is the busiest time of day for puffins. There are puffins carrying beakloads of fish for their chicks, puffins at their burrow entrances basking in the last rays of the setting sun, puffins squabbling with their neighbours, puffins preening, and puffins flying round and round in great circles above the colony.

Every summer Puffin Island is visited by a team of ornithologists from the IWC. We count the razorbills on the scree slopes, the guillemots and kittiwakes on their ledges on the steepest cliffs, the fulmars on their nests, to see if the populations are increasing or decreasing. We count the burrows occupied by puffins. We measure the growth rates of the puffin chicks and see what species of fish their parents are bringing them.

One of the main aims of the annual visit is to ring the birds. In the past few years nearly 3000 puffins have been ringed on the island. Each bird is marked with a numbered metal leg ring.

Fleyging puffins

Young puffins in their burrows are easy to catch for ringing if you don't mind getting very dirty — puffins don't keep their burrows very clean and tidy! The adults are caught as they fly past the cliffs, using a special net called a fleyg net. This is the traditional method of catching puffins (for eating!) in the Faeroe Islands. The fleyg net is like a large butterfly net and in skilled hands it can catch large numbers of puffins in a very short time. The bird is not harmed by the net. It is ringed, weighed and measured, and then quickly released. In spite of their friendly, comical appearance, puffins are fierce and strong. The ringer's hands are soon covered in bites and scratches. All in a day's work for a puffin ringer!

The puffin on the right is wearing a coloured plastic ring as well as the standard metal ring.

Once the puffin has been ringed and released it may be caught at another colony or perhaps found dead on a beach or in a fisherman's net. In this way we gather information on the movements of the birds.

Very few ringed puffins are ever found again once they have been released. Out of every thousand puffins ringed in Ireland and Britain, only eight are ever recovered. The number of recoveries from Puffin Island birds is even smaller — less than five out of every thousand. So we have to ring a lot of puffins to learn about their movements.

Most puffins are found very close to the colony. However, a puffin from Puffin Island was discovered one winter on the island of Sardinia in the Mediterranean Sea. From studies carried out elsewhere we know that most Irish puffins spend the winter in the Atlantic Ocean and off the coasts of France and Spain. So the one that went to Sardinia went a little further than usual.

BIRD RINGING

by Hugh Brazier

On pages 40 and 41 you can read how puffins are caught and ringed, and how ringing can tell us about their movements. But many other birds besides puffins are ringed in Ireland. Altogether about 35,000 birds are ringed here each year.

Most small birds are caught for ringing in very fine nets called mist nets. They are so fine that they are almost invisible. The bird does not see the net and flies into it. It gets entangled in the meshes of the net and there it lies safely until the ringer comes to extract it.

There are several different sizes of ring to fit all the different sizes of birds, from a goldcrest to a mute swan. Each ring has its own unique number, like a car registration number, and an address so that the person finding the ringed bird knows where to report the find.

How much does a ring weigh?

People often ask this question — maybe they are worried that the bird is weighed down by the ring. The ring is so light, in fact, that it makes no difference to the bird. It is made of extremely light but strong alloys of aluminium. The ring worn by a robin weighs 0.047 grams. It takes over 300 of them to equal the robin's own weight. The ring causes as little inconvenience to the bird as your wrist-watch does to you.

A female blackbird receives her ring

Movements and migrations

Ringing has revealed a lot about the migration of birds — but there is still much to be discovered. The recovery of a ringed bird is often exciting, maybe because the bird has travelled a long way or maybe because it has moved very fast. A storm petrel ringed at a colony in Donegal on 4 August 1980 was caught again only three days later by another ringer on Bardsey Island off the coast of north Wales. Another storm petrel took only four days to travel from St Kilda, off the west coast of Scotland, to Inismurray in County Sligo.

Sedge warblers on their autumn migration can also make some rapid movements. One bird ringed at Ballycotton in County Cork on 3 August 1984 was found near Bristol in England six days later.

Waders often travel very long distances. Dunlin from Germany, Norway, Sweden and Russia are regularly found on Irish estuaries in winter. Dunlin ringed in Ireland have turned up in France, Spain and Morocco.

Long-lived birds

Ringing tells us where birds go on migration, but it can also tell us a great deal more besides. For example, from ringing we can find out how long birds live. Here are some of the old-age records for birds ringed in Britain and Ireland. The figure shows the number of years that passed between ringing and recovery. The actual lifespans of the birds may have been longer.

Manx shearwater	30 years
Fulmar	27 years
Arctic tern	27 years
Razorbill	25 years
Curlew	24 years
Puffin	23 years
Mute swan	22 years
Blue tit	12 years
Dunnock	9 years
Willow warbler	8 years
Goldcrest	4 years

If you find a ringed bird . . .

As you explore the countryside or seashore — or the town — you will come across dead birds. Always check to see if a dead bird is ringed and sooner or later you will be lucky enough to find one that is. You should report your find to the address on the ring or to the British Trust for Ornithology, Beech Grove, Tring, Hertfordshire, England. Don't forget the following information:

1. the ring number
2. the date and place you found it
3. the species of bird, if you can identify it
4. whether the bird was found dead, killed by a cat, or any other circumstances surrounding the discovery
5. your name and address

If possible remove the ring from the bird and send the ring off along with your letter (tape it to the letter so that it doesn't get lost in the post!). If you see a ringed bird visiting your bird table DO NOT attempt to catch it to read the ring number. It would be illegal to do so and you might harm the bird. The best way of finding rings is to examine all the dead birds that you see.

If you report your find, in due course you will hear when and where your bird was ringed. And you will have the satisfaction of knowing that you have made a contribution to our knowledge of birds.

How can you become a ringer?

Ringing is a difficult art to master. A ringer must be able to handle all types of birds safely and must know how to identify the species, age and sex of every bird caught. All ringers must therefore hold a permit issued by the British Trust for Ornithology and in Ireland they must also have a licence from the Forest and Wildlife Service. In order to qualify as a ringer you must first undergo a rigorous training programme under the supervision of an experienced ringer. You must be fourteen years of age before you can start training. The Irish Wildbird Conservancy (Southview, Church Road, Greystones, County Wicklow) can supply you with a list of trainers in the Republic of Ireland.

Charles J. Haughey

Profile 5: The Politician
Interview by Deirdre Purcell

Every morning, when the Taoiseach leaves his Kinsealy home to travel into Dublin for the business of the day, he leaves a peaceful, pastoral oasis in the hurly-burly of his busy life.

On a sunny summer morning, two hares jump and play in the paddock right in front of his front door. An inquisitive robin perches in the ivy covering the front of the house. Blackbirds and thrushes sing in the huge spreading cedar on the driveway — and pairs of house martins swoop in and out of the stable yard. On a small lake, at the back of the house, there are mallard, coots and even a heron. A pair of swans have nested there for some years — and the surrounding woods are populated by deer.

The mallard and deer were introduced by the Haugheys and the former caused quite a problem. Mr Haughey knew that swans are very territorial and was worried that the male might object to the new arrivals, so he rang the zoo. He was told there would be no problem. But there was.

'I saw the male swan going up and down like a battleship, killing the little ducks.' The experience taught him two things. In the wild, creatures are individuals and may not conform to the 'normal' behaviour patterns of their species. And also, 'it is much more interesting to find things out for yourself through observation.' A book or an expert may help, but may not always know everything.

Mr Haughey grew up in the working class Dublin suburb of Donnycarney, then on the fringes of the city. Because money was scarce, the children of the area were by and large left to make their own entertainment. So he and his friends ambled across the fields close to their houses or travelled out to the seaside area of Howth, not far away. They absorbed the fact that the fields, headlands and strands they crossed were inhabited by creatures other than themselves. Having little money to spend on artificial pastimes like today's arcade games, they went searching for birds' nests. And, he admits regretfully, robbed them of their eggs. He would never condone that now, of course, but the practice did kindle a lifelong interest in wildlife.

He would not regard himself as 'intensely' interested. When on his holiday island of Inisvickillaun in County Kerry, he does not spend hours and hours just watching. He is too active for that. Instead, almost every day, he 'does a little recce'. (Short for a 'reconnaissance mission'. In military language it means scouting out the territory.)

'I do a little recce just to see how the deer are doing, or the hares . . . By the way, I believe that hares are the most beautiful animals of all . . .'

He introduced both species, deer and hare, to his island. 'When we went to Inisvickillaun first, the red deer in Killarney were under threat. These were the last of the native, purebred, Irish deer and there were only about 120 left in the herd.' The deer were threatened because they were breeding with the imported sika deer.

So he took a stag and three hinds out to his island, where they would be completely quarantined, free from any possibility of hybridisation, and they bred very successfully. Ironically, the move proved unnecessary 'because, as it happened, almost from that day on, the herd in Killarney started to come up again. Now it numbers almost six hundred.' And in fact some of the animals have now been transported to Connemara and to Doneraile, where it is hoped that new herds of native deer will become firmly established.

Mr Haughey firmly believes that wildlife and the environment are vital components in the heritage of Ireland. He sees these issues as part of a span which covers architecture and archaeology as well. His plan is that a totally new body called the National Heritage Council will supervise affairs in this area.

But he emphasises that all the official bodies and committees or councils in the world will be ineffectual, no matter how hard they try, if the ordinary members of the public do not come to see that preserving their environment and their heritage starts with themselves. 'The only way you'll preserve the environment, wildlife and our archaeological heritage, is with public opinion. They are the only people who can actually do it, that's where it begins. The state can't stop people robbing crosses — but the public can . . .'

He is aware of the pressures. 'All the pressures are for amenities and facilities, for economic development and jobs.' He has sympathy for the local concern in an economically deprived area, which would encourage Bord na Móna, for instance, to develop a bog in order to provide a hundred jobs for ten years.

On the other hand, once that bog is 'developed', it is dead. The wildlife it supported, perhaps for thousands of years, will have disappeared for ever.

Sometimes, of course, we find that we have little control over our environment. There was a wonderful story in Wexford, on the famous Slobs. These came up for sale and there was a strong push that the land should be put to progressive use for modern farming. Naturally, environmentalists were appalled, since the Slobs are one of the most important wintering areas in Europe for geese.

Solomon-like, a solution was found. The state bought half the land to preserve it for the geese, while a local farmer bought the other half. He planted it with wheat.

'The geese came along and looked down from the sky. "Oh what a nice man! Planting all that lovely wheat for us to eat!" It was just coming up, lovely and green and luscious . . .'

The poor man persevered for a few years but got fed up with providing free eats for winter visitors and finally sold off his 'progressive' farm. Mr Haughey has sympathy for the farmer, but *loves* the story.

He believes a balance must be struck. For instance, with regard to the water-bus controversy in Killarney, where purists insist that even one water-bus filled with tourists, plying the lakes, will wreak havoc on the environment, Mr Haughey is on the side of the water-bus. 'People get hysterical about things like this. I believe that the ordinary person should have as much right to see the Lakes of Killarney like they've never been seen before, as do these people who want to keep the amenities to themselves, purer than pure.'

He considers himself to be in the forefront of the anti-nuclear lobby. 'I'm very anti-nuclear. It horrifies me, terrifies me.' He got 'very very upset' at the time of the nuclear accident at Chernobyl, when he heard about the advice being given to children all over the continent of Europe. 'When we were children, we were always being told, "eat up your green vegetables! Go out and get some fresh air!" After Chernobyl, these were the things that the children in Europe were told *not* to do. They were told, "stay indoors because the air is bad for you. Don't eat vegetables because they're poisoned . . .".'

But a Taoiseach of Ireland, even though a man of influence at home and in Europe, has little influence when it comes to the nuclear power games being played by the super-powers. He knows this but is committed to try to use all the influence at his disposal.

He will use his influence within Ireland. And he hopes that wildlife and environmental issues will gain more prominence on the school curriculum. He would welcome initiatives in this area. 'This is where it all has to start — in the schools.'

He knows he is lucky in his own environment, both at home in Kinsealy and on Inisvickillaun, particularly in the latter. 'There, you feel at the heart of things, more human, at ease. In the city, you're busy, you're engaged, you're preoccupied, worried, anxious, fussed.'

As he drives towards the heart of the city each morning, he passes within yards of his old home in Donnycarney, now no longer on the dividing line between field and city, but engulfed by sprawling newer and bigger suburbs. He passes Darndale and Coolock, economically deprived and suffering chronically from unemployment and other ailments of modern Ireland.

But even there the birds still sing and foxes have been known to prey on dustbins. And from the dual carriageway which speeds the traffic past them can be seen the encircling blue mountains of Dublin and Wicklow.

Is the Water Clean?

Unfortunately we hear a lot about water pollution. Many plants and animals live in and on rivers, lakes and ponds. Most of them need clean water. If the water is polluted many plants and animals die.

But how can you tell if the pond or river near your home is clean or polluted?

1. Use this checklist:

Signs of cleanness	Signs of pollution
looks clean	looks dirty
no litter on surface	litter on surface
no oil	oil on surface
water clear	water cloudy
plenty of water life	few or no signs of life

2. Study the animals living in the water

You will need:
- a pond net
- a large light-coloured plastic container — an ice cream or margarine tub is ideal

What to do:

Sweep the net *quickly* and firmly through the water. It is no good doing it slowly. (What would you do if you saw or felt a monstrous pond net approaching?)

You will get your best catches near the bottom and in clumps of vegetation, which is where most of the invertebrates live.

Empty your catch by turning your net inside out in some clean water in your container.

You may see nothing at first. Let things settle and look carefully, and you will see things crawling about.

When you have finished examining your catch, tip the animals back into the pond.

When you visit a pond or river
- always take a friend with you
- always tell an adult where you are going and when you expect to be back

Identification chart for water pollution

Pollution level A — very clean water

If you find these animals, the water is very clean

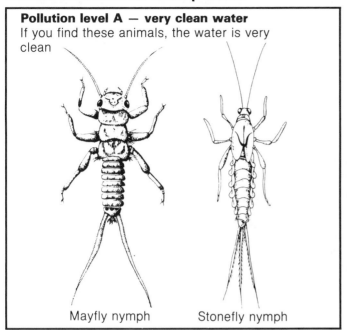

Mayfly nymph   Stonefly nymph

Pollution level B — slightly dirty water

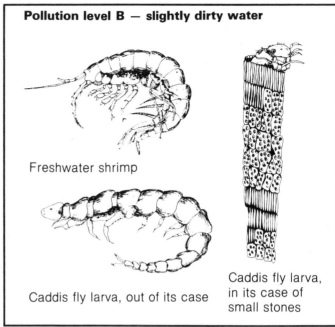

Freshwater shrimp

Caddis fly larva, out of its case

Caddis fly larva, in its case of small stones

Pollution level C — very dirty water

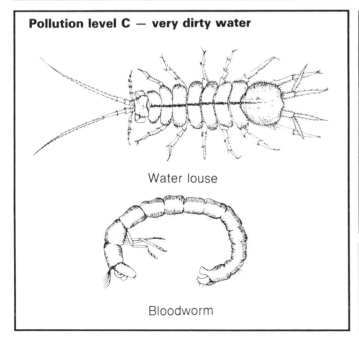

Water louse

Bloodworm

Pollution level D — extremely polluted

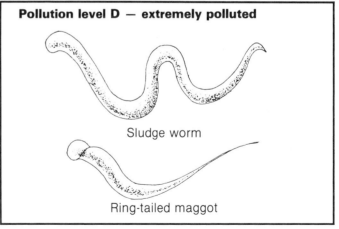

Sludge worm

Ring-tailed maggot

Pollution level E — dead

If you find no visible sign of life, call this pollution level E

NEW RESEARCH ON NATURE IN IRELAND
compiled by Richard Nairn

INSECTS GO TO SEA

Many insects are blown out to sea and end up floating on the waves. Here they join the plankton which is formed of tiny marine animals and plants and they become a source of food for surface living fish. The commonest floating insects in Irish waters are two-winged flies and winged aphids (or greenfly). Beetles,

Oil beetle

ants, wasps, midges and many other insects have been found floating at sea. Most are poor flyers and cannot resist the strong winds which carry them to their fate. Garfish are especially fond of scooping insects off the surface of the sea. (DeCourcy Williams and Dorman, *Irish Naturalists' Journal* 1986)

Wasp

PIED FLYCATCHERS ARRIVE

Up to 1985 pied flycatchers were only seen in Ireland on migration, appearing on offshore islands and headlands. In Britain they are quite common breeding birds in oakwoods along upland river valleys where they nest in holes in old trees. Very little native oakwood survives in Ireland and most of what remains is formed of young trees with few natural holes. Nestboxes were erected in suitable woods in counties Antrim and Wicklow and in 1985 for the first time ever pied flycatchers nested successfully in Ireland. Unfortunately the young flycatchers in the Wicklow nestboxes were eaten by an unidentified predator. (Bradley and Fagan, *Irish Birds* 1986)

Pied flycatcher

CLARE ISLAND REVISITED

The Clare Island Survey of 1909-11 was one of the greatest works of natural history ever carried out in Ireland. As a result of the work of many famous naturalists of the early twentieth century, led by Robert Lloyd Praeger, this west coast island is one of the best studied areas in the country. Now, after almost eighty years, Clare Island's plants have been surveyed again and a major change has been found. The change from crop growing to sheep grazing has led to the disappearance of many wild flowers of the cornfields.

Clare Island

Overgrazing has destroyed much of the woodland causing more wild flowers to be lost. Most of the new plants found in this survey were introduced or had escaped from gardens. (Doyle and Foss, *Irish Naturalists' Journal* 1986)

Bank vole

OWLS AND VOLES

Barn owls are widespread in Ireland, and hunt by night in both town and country areas. They feed mainly on a variety of small mammals including rats, mice and shrews, with occasional birds, frogs, bats and beetles when these are available. In the south-west of Ireland a new mammal, the bank vole, was introduced sometime before 1964 and these little animals now make up about one-fifth of the owl's diet in this area. The bank vole prefers thicker cover than the field mouse so is probably less easy for the owls to catch. In poorer habitats such as rough grass or moorland, where the rodents become scarce, the owls turn to feeding on birds, frogs, pygmy shrews and other prey. Perhaps the addition of the bank vole to its diet will help the owls to increase. (Smal, *Bird Study* 1987)

STAY-AT-HOME HERONS

Despite their wingspan of up to two metres herons are not long distance flyers, especially in Ireland. Over two-thirds of herons ringed at nests in Connemara have been recovered within twenty kilometres of the nest site and the only long distance movements involved young birds blown by gale-force winds and later found dead or dying. The wet conditions in western Ireland provide an abundance of food for herons at all times of the year. Because winter frosts are rare on the west coast there is no need for herons to migrate south in winter to avoid frozen water and starvation. Although most of the herons in Connemara nest on islands in freshwater lakes, they fly to the nearby coast to feed on fish and crabs among the rock pools and seaweed. Only the young birds fly away to find new breeding areas but many do not survive. Most die of natural causes but some are shot or collide with overhead wires. (Partridge, *Irish Birds* 1986)

Heron

VISITORS TO THE FLAG

The yellow flag or iris is a common and attractive flower of wet fields, ditches and marshes throughout Ireland. Like many other plants its pollen is carried from one flower to the next by visiting insects such as bees which come to feed on nectar. Bumble bees and hoverflies are the commonest daytime visitors to the flag with moths calling in at night. One type of hoverfly is only common where there are plenty of cattle because its larvae live in cow dung.

Yellow flag

Because the hoverfly is much smaller than the bee it does not pick up much pollen from the stamens of the flower and may not be much help to the plant. However, as the flower gets older the space inside gets less and the fly may touch the stamens more. The lower petals of the flag have striking patterns which may help to guide the insect visitors in to the pollen. (Good, *Irish Naturalists' Journal* 1986)

Make a Leaf Hedgehog

You will need

A collection of dead leaves of different
   shapes and colours
Newspaper
Heavy books for pressing the leaves
Thick paper or card for the background
Scissors
Glue
Felt-tip pens, paints or crayons
Clear film or PVA glue

What to do

Make sure all the leaves are clean and dry,
then place them carefully between several
layers of newspaper. Make sure they do not
overlap. Use some heavy books to weigh
down the newspaper. Press the leaves for
several days.

Cut out some card in the shape of a
hedgehog, and arrange the leaves on it. Use
spiky leaves, such as willow, to make the
hedgehog's spines. Fill in the rest of the
body with leaves of different shapes. When
you are happy that your hedgehog looks
right, stick down the leaves.

Complete the hedgehog by drawing in
whiskers, mouth, an eye, and toes.

The picture will last longer if you cover it
with clear film or varnish it with a thin coat
of PVA glue diluted in water.

How many other animals can you make out
of dead leaves? Try a lion (with a shaggy
mane) or a squirrel (with a bushy tail).

Can you name all the leaves you have
collected?

STREET-WISE

Do you think wildlife is only found in the countryside? If you live in a town or city, look around you and you might be surprised at what you can see.

- How many animals can you find in the city?
- Where do they live?
- What do they eat?

You might see foxes, rats, mice, hedgehogs, bats, and even badgers. But most mammals are only active at night, and they are very shy and hard to see. So you probably won't see many even if they are there.

Birds are much easier to see. They are active during the day and many of them don't seem to mind people too much, so you can get close to them and see what they are doing.

Choose a quiet street. The best times to work are in the early morning and in the late afternoon. Birds often rest at midday. WATCH OUT FOR TRAFFIC! Walk along the street very quietly looking for birds. Use a table like the one below for recording where you see them. Put a tick each time you see a bird. Do different birds use different parts of the street?

Food for birds
- **Rubbish** — Many of the street birds are scavengers, living on rubbish. Examine the litter in the city and make a list of any foods that birds could eat. Which birds do you see feeding on rubbish? WARNING — do not touch the litter with your hands. Use a stick to sort it out.

	road	gutter	pavement	trees	grass	gardens	buildings	sky
house sparrow								
feral pigeon								
wood pigeon								
blackbird								
jackdaw								
magpie								
starling								
black-headed gull								
swift								
others								

- **Garden plants and trees** — Examine the plants and trees that you see in gardens. List any foods that could be eaten by birds, such as seeds and berries. Which birds do you see feeding here?
- **Wild plants** — Many wild plants grow in the street. Most people call them weeds and think they are worthless. In fact they can be an important source of food for city birds. Which birds do you see feeding on wild plants? What part of the plants are they eating? Or are they feeding on insects on the plants?
- **Insects** — Birds hunt insects and other mini-beasts. These are especially important in spring and summer when birds are feeding their young. Look for habitats that attract mini-beasts. Try to name the mini-beasts that you find.

WASTELAND

Many plots of land in town are not at present used by people. Some are places where an old house has been knocked down and nothing has yet been built in its place. Maybe the owners of the site are waiting for money or planning permission before rebuilding.

Wild plants and animals do not wait for funds or planning permission before moving in, so on most wasteland there is wildlife. In fact, a recent study in Dublin found that wasteland is one of the best places in a city for birds.

Study some wasteland near your home or your school. As you work, watch out for broken glass, old tin cans and other dangers.

How long has your wasteland been unoccupied?
You can find out by asking people in the area. Better still, study the vegetation on the wasteland. If bushes and trees have grown up, it has probably been empty for some years. If there are no bushes or trees, it may have been empty for only a year or two.

Homes for wildlife — habitats
A patch of waste ground, like any other piece of ground, is likely to provide lots of different homes for many different plants and animals. Tick any of the following which are available for wildlife:

broken down walls   long grass
bare earth   wild flowers
old sheds   trees
water in pond or ditch   bushes
rubbish tip

Wasteland flowers

Compare the flowers on the wasteland with those you find beside the road or at the edges of fields. Are the same plants growing there?

Wasteland is quite a difficult environment for plants. Often the soil is rather dry. Sometimes there is very little earth and the plants can only put down roots in cracks between stones or concrete. The first plants to arrive in 'new' wasteland are often those whose seeds are blown by the wind, for example Oxford ragwort, rosebay willowherb, dandelion, groundsel and thistle.

Look for garden plants which may have survived from previous gardens on the site, or may have spread from nearby gardens. Sometimes you may find young apple trees — or even orange trees — which have grown from pips left by picnickers.

Wasteland birds

Walk round the area quietly and make a list of any birds you see. Look for nests in bushes, trees, cracks in walls or even on the ground. Never touch a nest or make a noise which might disturb nesting birds.

Which is the commonest wasteland bird? Have you seen any bird here which you do not often see in streets or gardens?

Wasteland mammals

Look out for signs of mammals too. Make notes about any droppings, footprints or tunnels in the undergrowth which suggest that wild mammals use the land.

Wasteland minibeasts

Investigate the insect life of the wasteland. Make a list of all the insects and other mini-beasts which you find. Which plants are best for insects?

FIND OUT ABOUT HEDGEROWS

In prehistoric times Ireland was covered by forests, and many of our plants and animals are adapted to life in a woodland environment. Over the last seven thousand years the forests have been cleared to make way for fields. Life has got harder for the woodland creatures. Open fields are no good to them.

After clearing the forests, however, farmers in Ireland started planting hedges to stop their animals straying. There is now a network of hedgerows across much of the country. These hedgerows are like miniature woods, and are now an important refuge for the plants and animals which once lived in the primeval forests. Plants like blackberry, primrose, bluebell and wood sorrel are now found in hedges as well as in woodland.

The centre of a wood is often rather dark. Not enough light penetrates through the canopy of trees, and few shrubs and flowering plants can grow there. At the edge of a wood, however, the habitat is much richer. Plenty of light means that more plants can grow, and the insects, birds and mammals are also more abundant at the edge of a wood. A hedgerow is like a woodland edge with no wood attached — an especially valuable habitat.

Hedgerows are not very old compared with many other features of the landscape. Most Irish hedges are probably no more than a few hundred years old.

In different parts of the country there are different types of hedgerow. In the fertile lowlands of Leinster many hedges are quite tall, and trees like hawthorn, ash, beech, sycamore and elder are common. On the poorer soil of more mountainous areas the typical shrubs and trees of hedges include gorse, holly, hazel, ash, hawthorn and birch. In the west of Ireland, fuchsia hedges, full of red flowers, are very common.

Hedges are now under threat. Many hedges are being destroyed to make bigger fields, or are being replaced by barbed-wire fences.

How old is the hedge?

When you begin to inspect hedges in the countryside you will see that they are much more varied and interesting than the typical privet hedge of a suburban garden. But some are more varied than others. Some hedges contain almost nothing but hawthorn, but others have many different kinds of woody shrubs and trees in them.

You can use the woody shrubs to tell you how old a hedge is. As a hedge gets older, it becomes more varied.

Why not compare two different hedges, and see which of them is the older? Choose one roadside hedge and one hedge between fields.

1. Divide each hedge up into thirty-metre lengths. Use sticks to mark the lengths.

2. Walk slowly down each length and count how many different kinds of woody plants are growing in it. You don't need to know the names of all of them. Count trees in your total but do not count ivy, honeysuckle or other woody climbers. Also ignore brambles.

3. Find the average number of kinds of woody shrub growing in a thirty-metre length of the hedge.

4. Compare the results from the two hedges. Which hedge is older? You could do a survey of many different hedges. You could learn a lot about the history of your local area from this project.

How many of these trees and shrubs can you find growing in hedges?

Ash	Elm	Oak
Beech	Fuchsia	Privet
Birch	Gorse	Rose
Blackthorn	Hawthorn	Sycamore
Crab Apple	Hazel	Willow
Elder	Holly	

In some parts of England it has been found that the number of different woody plants in a hedge, multiplied by one hundred, is equal to the age of the hedge in years. A hedge that is three hundred years old has about three species of tree or shrub in each thirty-metre length, and a hedge five hundred years old has about five.

Be a Plant Scientist

by Jim Hurley

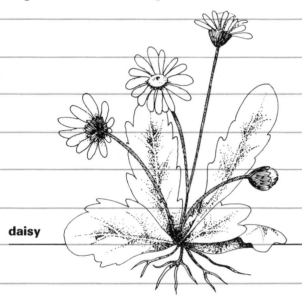

daisy

Object — To find out how common daisies are in a lawn.

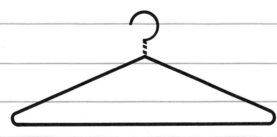

Method — Get one of the wire coat hangers used by dry cleaners and bend it

into a square. Scientists call this square a QUADRAT FRAME. Tie a coloured ribbon on it so that it won't get lost in the grass.

Stand anywhere on the lawn. Check that there is nobody behind you, then fling the quadrat frame over your shoulder and follow it to where it lands. You are now going to look in detail at the small patch of ground within your frame. Scientists call this a RANDOM SAMPLE of the lawn.

The quadrat was thrown at random on the lawn, but it missed because Random ducked!

Study the ground carefully, and count the daisies within the frame. When flowers are absent in winter, or after mowing, you can still do this project by looking for the rosettes of daisy leaves. See how many daisies are within the frame and decide from the following table which number you will give it.

Number	How common daisies are
0	ABSENT (no daisies at all)
1	RARE (one or two daisies)
2	SCARCE (only a few daisies)
3	COMMON (a good number of daisies)
4	VERY COMMON (many daisies)
5	ABUNDANT (full of daisies)

Plant scientists call these numbers the ABUNDANCE CLASS.

Repeat the throwing exercise ten times. Copy out this table and fill in your results.

Quadrat number	Abundance class
1	
2	
3	
4	
5	
6	
7	
8	
9	
10	
Total	
Average $\left(\dfrac{\text{total}}{10}\right)$	

When you add up your numbers and divide the total by ten the answer tells you whether daisies are common or scarce in your lawn. The experiment can be repeated on other lawns and the results compared.

DO YOU KNOW YOUR BINDWEEDS?

by Jim Hurley

I'm sure you know the hedge bindweed — that persistent climbing weed often seen in hedgerows and waste places, sporting its large waxy-white, trumpet-shaped flowers. But did you know that there are six different kinds of bindweed in Ireland? Perhaps you could watch out for them next summer and make a point of examining each of them in its natural surroundings.

Five climbers, one crawler

Five of our bindweeds are climbers and have arrow shaped leaves, so it is easy to recognise the odd one out, the *sea bindweed,* because it creeps flat on the ground, does not twine around other plants, has fleshy kidney shaped leaves and lives on sandy ground near the sea. The bell-like flowers are an attractive pale pink colour with five white stripes.

Clockwise or anticlockwise?

When you come to sort out the five climbing bindweeds you should look first at the way the stems twine as they climb. If they twine clockwise, and are angled, your plant is *black bindweed.* It has small greenish-pink flowers and grows in sandy places and as a weed of cultivated ground. Though it looks like a bindweed it is really a member of the dock family.

Small bracts . . .

The stems of the true bindweeds all twine anti-clockwise. If you study the base of one of the bell-shaped flowers you may notice two large, broad, pointed leaf-like structures. These are not true leaves but are called bracts. The only true bindweed with tiny bracts is the *field bindweed.* It is also the only one with scented flowers. The flowers are often pink but they may have white stripes or be all-white.

. . . and big bracts

The remaining three bindweeds all have big bracts. As its name tells you the *hairy bindweed* is the only hairy one. It is not very hairy but you should be able to see some hairs on the stalks of the leaves and the bright pink

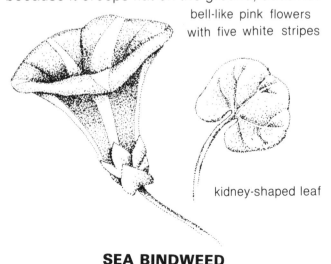

bell-like pink flowers
with five white stripes

kidney-shaped leaf

SEA BINDWEED

flowers. It is a garden escapee so it is only found scrambling through hedges near houses.

The *large bindweed* is larger in all its parts and has flowers up to 75mm across. One of its key features is that the bracts are very swollen and they overlap at the base. It is also a garden escapee that may be found near houses.

Commonest of all

The sixth bindweed, the *hedge bindweed,* is not hairy, its flowers are never more than 50mm across and its bracts are not swollen and do not overlap. It is very common in hedges and thickets. The flowers are usually white, but a pink form has been found in south Kerry, west Cork, Clare and west Galway. Though not scented the flowers are attractive to bumble bees, hoverflies and the convolvulus hawk moth.

Key to bindweeds

1. Leaves kidney-shaped . . . sea bindweed /Clamhán/*Calystegia soldanella*
   Leaves arrow-shaped . . . 2.

2. Stems twine clockwise . . . black bindweed /Glúineach dhubh/*Fallopia convolvulus*
   Stems twine anti-clockwise . . . 3.

3. Bracts tiny . . . field bindweed/Ainleog/*Convolvulus arvensis*
   Bracts big . . . 4.

4. Hairy . . . hairy bindweed/Ialus giobach/*Calystegia pulchra*
   Not hairy . . . 5.

5. Bracts swollen . . . large bindweed/Ialus mór/ *Calystegia silvatica*

6. Bracts not swollen . . . hedge bindweed/Ialus fáil/ *Calystegia sepium*

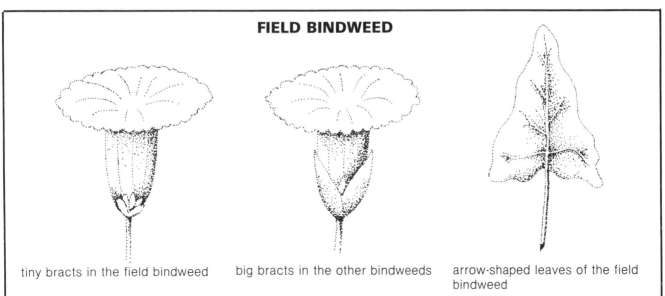

FIELD BINDWEED

tiny bracts in the field bindweed

big bracts in the other bindweeds

arrow-shaped leaves of the field bindweed

Voyage Underwater

by Jim Hurley

In last year's *Wildlife Book* we told you how to set up a jam jar aquarium. Did you set one up? How did it work out for you? An aquarium is a valuable tool for studying freshwater wildlife, but a much more exciting thing to do is to travel underwater in a real pond and to meet the creatures face to face in their natural surroundings. You don't need a submarine or scuba gear — all you need is an underwater viewer.

You can easily make a viewer, as shown in the diagram.

The cling film is easy to tear so it is a good idea to bring a box of spare film with you. You should also bring a pair of scissors, a few rubber bands and a plastic bag to put your rubbish in so that you can bring it home with you.

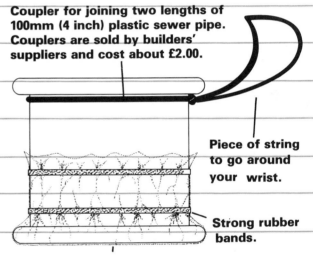

Coupler for joining two lengths of 100mm (4 inch) plastic sewer pipe. Couplers are sold by builders' suppliers and cost about £2.00.

Piece of string to go around your wrist.

Strong rubber bands.

Self-adhesive cling film used for wrapping food.

- Bring a friend with you to hold your legs and see that you don't fall in.
- Tell an adult where you are going and when you will be back.
- Do not cause any upset to the creatures you have come to visit.
- Bring your litter home with you.

At the pond . . .

Pick a well-lit, shallow place to examine the underwater life. Your viewer will do away with any glare or choppiness on the water surface.

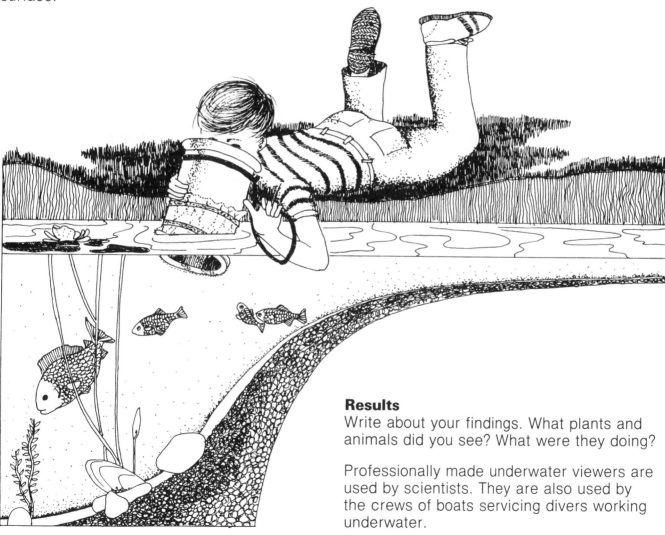

Results

Write about your findings. What plants and animals did you see? What were they doing?

Professionally made underwater viewers are used by scientists. They are also used by the crews of boats servicing divers working underwater.

How You Can Help Wildlife in Your Garden

How many of these features does your garden have? See what you can do to help the wildlife in your area.

1 and 2 COMPOST HEAP AND LOG PILES
Provide grubs and insects for birds such as robins, wrens and blackbirds. Offer a home for hedgehogs.

3 NETTLES
Provide a breeding ground for small tortoiseshell, peacock and red admiral butterflies.

4 and 5 SUNFLOWERS AND TEAZLES
Attract colourful seed-eating birds such as goldfinches.

6 LONG GRASS
Attracts butterflies and other insects.

7 SHRUBS
Those bearing berries, such as cotoneaster or berberis, give colour in autumn and provide food for the birds.

8 A POND
Makes a home for frogs, attracts dragonflies and provides a drinking place for birds.

9 NECTAR-RICH PLANTS
Buddleia, yellow alyssum, sweet rocket, lavender, honesty, thyme and sedum attract a host of butterflies.

10 NEST BOXES
Should be placed out of reach of cats, facing roughly north-east — never facing south into the hot midday sun.

11 HONEYSUCKLE
Provides good nesting sites and food for birds. It also attracts moths.

Declan Doogue

Profile 6: The Botanist
Interview by Deirdre Purcell

The young Declan Doogue — already a botanist.

Declan Doogue is not all that interested in going to study the lush flora in a place like the Amazon rain forests. They do nothing at all for him. Ireland has so much to offer — he is only *beginning* to come to grips with it all — and it has quite enough, thank you, for a lifetime's study.

'I think there's so much to learn and to see in Ireland. I'm only getting to the stage now where if you put me in a field somewhere I could make a reasonably good guess where I am. I could probably work it out from the flora and the fauna and a little bit of soil information as well.'

When he was a child in Finglas, Dublin, Declan, who is now a national school teacher with a class of forty-two eight and nine-year-olds, built himself a little toy zoo and stocked it with live creatures from his back garden. In his imagination, the garden snails were his tortoises and the earthworms were his venomous snakes. (His mother's reaction to the 'zoo' is not recorded.)

And Wednesdays were special days. It was on Wednesdays that the flickering black and white images of David Attenborough's television series such as *Zoo Quest in Guyana* and *Zoo Quest in Paraguay* were transmitted. His father, a civil servant, worked late on Wednesdays so Declan had the television to himself. After homework of course.

He believes that true naturalists are born, not made. No amount of teaching or urging can sow interest where none naturally exists. What can be done, however, is to release that interest. As Chairman of the Dublin Naturalists' Field Club, he leads lots of excursions into the largely unknown world of nature around and in our capital city. 'People just don't see certain things. You might be pointing to something the size of a penguin and they just can't see it.'

So people take a springtime drive into the Burren in County Clare, a botanist's paradise. They go because they know it is the correct thing to do. 'And you say to them when they come back: "what did you see?"'

"Oh, we saw the gentians. Yes. Wonderful show altogether."

"Anything else?"

"No, not really, but the scenery was great," or "the weather was lovely," or "we had a grand time in Doolin."
People go out into the countryside and they come back with very little.'

He points out that during the course of a short country walk in County Dublin you can find between 110 and 120 species of flowering plants in the roadside verges, 'including the hedgerow, the bit of field at the back, maybe a weedy patch in someone's garden'. Most people, while strolling along, or even looking, would not see a tenth of that number of species. 'Part of the problem is that filters are always operating. People look at a piece of scenery and they see mountains or lakes, but not the seal or the rabbit which might be only five metres away from them.'

The difficulty lies in shattering the filters and clearing the images. He does it by having people get right down on their hands and knees, to turn over stones or feel the texture of the plants. 'When you have them doing that and picking up flowers and making close comparisons — then suddenly the information is absorbed.'

As for the children he teaches — Declan has them lying on their bellies in a city park in the middle of winter, for instance, searching under the park railings for hibernating ladybirds. But he also encourages them to start collections. 'Kids love collecting things — they collect stones, postcards, football cards — anything at all. And they love bringing things in and wanting to know what they are. It only takes one kid to bring something in and if there is any sort of reasonable feedback, then somebody else will bring in something the next day.' Of course this technique has its disadvantages too. He had just found himself appointed doctor to a baby hooded crow which had fallen out of a nest. 'When you get the name for being good at that sort of thing, every unfortunate half-dead animal is lugged in.'

Among his pupils, he can spot the potential naturalists quite easily. He can split his class into two groups. The larger group consists of sportsmen, who are mainly interested in physical activity, in being healthy, in competing and winning. The other group, to which he belonged himself as a child, is more quiet and thoughtful.

Declan says that part of the problem in making natural history more popular is its genteel image, which still hangs over from the days when collecting wild flowers and pressing them was a pastime for elderly ladies dressed in sensible tweed skirts. 'These were the type of people who were recording and studying natural history in Ireland in the 1880s and 1890s. They were very productive people, very brilliant, but that particular scientific grouping kept very much to itself.'

He can remember exactly when his interest turned away from snails, slugs, earthworms and David Attenborough — and towards plants. He was foraging around in the basement of Eason's bookshop in Dublin. At the time, Eason's basement was a treasure house of secondhand books. He was browsing through a botany book and saw a rare plant called trueswort illustrated. Three weeks later, he was walking in the fields behind his house in Finglas when, lo and behold, he spotted the plant.

By coincidence, the following day a neighbour took him on a visit to the museum, where upstairs in the botany section he saw the plant again. He asked the attendant if the plant he had seen growing wild in Finglas could possibly be the same one. The attendant did not know, but advised him to come back the following Wednesday.

This he did, having picked his precious plant and put it in a jam jar. When he got to the museum he met a lady called Maura Scannell, who made a great fuss of him and his discovery and put him in touch with the Dublin Naturalists' Field Club, where he was also hailed as a great discoverer. From then on, he was hooked.

The next step was to join an organisation called The Botanical Society of the British Isles, quite a prestigious organisation, which had taken responsibility for classifying and cataloguing all the plants of Britain and Ireland, county by county. While he was still in secondary school, Declan, who had become 'pretty good at identifying plants', was given responsibility for recording the flora of all of County Kildare. It was a laborious job, involving not only field work, but also painstaking typing up of index cards. As a result of all this work, anyone who wanted to know where each sycamore tree grew in County Kildare, or where all the violets were dying off, could consult the files of Declan Doogue, official recorder of Kildare.

But why is all this so important?

'Number one, it helps you to "read" what you're in. It's like pages of a book. You go out into the countryside and suddenly you say "gosh! I'm on a bit of lime-rich grassland", or something like that. But you can read far more than that. You can say, "there was cultivation here up to about fifteen or twenty years ago". Over there, you can see where the lazy beds were. Look at the way the heather only grows on top of the ridges. You can look around and find the history of that particular field.'

There is great excitement in this, but also the intangible — the reason naturalists like Declan are born and not made. To him, identifying the topography of a place is as important as a work of art. 'In identifying it, I get the same buzz as you would from writing a poem. Something you're satisfied with.'

Declan Doogue believes in looking closely at the world around him.

The study of natural history has other advantages, such as the fresh air, the relaxation, the peaceful solitude. There is also the satisfaction of the hunter instinct. To the botanist, as to the wildlife photographer, sound recordist and ranger, finding and recording different species of plant life fulfils a primitive need. Some people want to shoot and kill something. Some people, like Declan Doogue, want to be able to *find* something.